# WHY SHOULD I GO TO COPENHAGEN

# WHY SHOULD I GO TO ↓
# COPENHAGEN

THE CITY YOU DEFINITELY
NEED TO VISIT
BEFORE YOU TURN 30 (OR 130)

HYTTEFADET

# THIS IS WHY!

Copenhagen is one of our favourite Nordic cities: it's calm and lively at the same time, and nice and close to the water. The city radiates green and sustainable living, with numerous parks, endless bike lanes, and eco-friendly innovations. One example is CopenHill, an energy plant that doubles as an artificial ski slope.

In Scandinavia, almost everything is a bit more expensive (to put it mildly), but with a few tips and tricks, visiting Copenhagen doesn't have to break the bank. Explore the different areas, avoid the tourist crowd at Nyhavn, and head to the neighbourhood of Nørrebro. Take in the scenery and soak up the atmosphere – that's what we love to do too.

Instead of going out for dinner, treat yourself to a fancy lunch and end the day with pizza or other street food. Wait for the sunset at Reffen or blend in with the locals at Dronning Louises Bro. Book a nice hostel, make sure to rent a bike, and visit museums like Ny Carlsberg Glyptotek, the wonderful Designmuseum, or Lykkemuseet (museum of happiness). Make sure to visit the flea markets and vintage shops as well: you're bound to find treasures of a lifetime.

Whether you're into culture, delicious food, or simply the vibe of an energetic city, Copenhagen has it all. Discover it for yourself and let the city inspire you. One thing is certain, you will want to come back for more. And more.

# CONTENTS

J. ALTHEN'S
SKRÄDDERI - AFFÄR
GUST. WOLKE
GLAS
KFC

Falafel 75.-/
Egg 65.-/
Grilled chicken

NORDIC HOTDOG

PHAGO

POW POW POW
SAMLEDE DIGTE
Syv rejste sten
SARA BAUME
GYSERHISTORIER

# NEIGHBOURHOODS

Copenhagen is divided into several areas that can be recognised by their names as well as their postcodes. First-time visitors will generally start in København K. But don't forget to explore other areas too. Due to its compact size, you'll quickly get to know the city.

**Indre By – København K (1000-1473)**

Indre By (meaning: inner city), also known as København K, is the vibrant heart of Copenhagen. This bustling neighbourhood is home to many of the city's most iconic landmarks, including the historic Tivoli Gardens, the picturesque harbour Nyhavn, and the grand Christiansborg Palace. Indre By, with its charming cobblestone streets, diverse shopping options, and array of restaurants, cafés, and bars is perfect for those who love to explore on foot. Whether you're interested in history, culture, or simply soaking up the urban atmosphere, Indre By has something for everyone.

**Vesterbro – København V (1500-1799)**

Once a gritty, working-class district, Vesterbro has transformed into one of the trendiest neighbourhoods. Known for its vibrant nightlife, eclectic mix of bars, restaurants, and cafés, Vesterbro attracts a diverse crowd. The Meatpacking District (Kødbyen) is a particular hotspot, bustling with trendy eateries and art galleries. Vesterbro is a lively area that perfectly balances its edgy past with a modern vibe.

NORDVEST
ØSTERBRO
ØRESUND
NØRREBRO
INDRE BY
FREDERIKSBERG
VESTERBRO
& SYDHAVN

### Frederiksberg (2000)

Frederiksberg is a charming and quiet residential area, known for its blend of urban design and nature. Although it's an independent municipality, it is entirely surrounded by the city of Copenhagen, which is why it is sometimes referred to as a city in the city, which also characteries its distinctive identity and it perfectly combines the energy of the city with the peace and quiet of the suburbs.

### Østerbro – København Ø (2100)

Østerbro is one of the city's more upscale and quiet neighbourhoods, known for its leafy lanes, elegant architecture, and proximity to the beautiful Fælledparken park. It's a family-friendly area with plenty of green spaces, playgrounds, and a variety of cafés and boutiques. Østerbro offers a mix of modern and historic attractions, including the iconic Little Mermaid statue and the impressive Kastellet fortress. This neighbourhood is perfect if you are looking to enjoy a more relaxed and refined side of the city.

### Nørrebro – København N (2200)

Nørrebro is a dynamic and multicultural neighbourhood pulsing with energy. Known for its diverse community, Nørrebro is a melting pot of cultures, reflected in its wide variety of restaurants offering global cuisines. The area is famous for its creative scene, with numerous independent boutiques and art galleries, as well as vibrant street art. Key highlights include the Assistens Cemetery, where famous Danes like Hans Christian Andersen are buried, and the

Superkilen park, a unique public space celebrating global diversity.

**Nordvest – København NV (2400)**

Nordvest is a rapidly developing area, known for its mix of old industrial buildings and new housing developments. The neighbourhood is attracting a creative crowd, and spots like Flere Fugle – a bakery, café, and pizza place – are popular among the city's creative communities. Rentemestervej is a notable street, blending historical charm and modern innovation, making Nordvest an exciting place to explore.

**Sydhavn – København S (2300 & 2450)**

Sydhavn, or South Harbour, is an evolving neighbourhood with a blend of contemporary buildings and historical sites, waterfront views and an increasing number of trendy cafés and shops. Sydhavn is perfect for those looking to experience a less touristy side of Copenhagen, with ample opportunities for waterfront dips and local dining.

**Hellerup/Charlottenlund/Klampenborg – Storkøbenhavn (2900, 2920 & 2930)**

Located just north of central Copenhagen, the areas of Hellerup, Charlottenlund, and Klampenborg offer a glimpse into the more affluent side of Danish life. Known for their beautiful residential streets, upscale shops, and proximity to the coast, these neighbourhoods are ideal if you are seeking a peaceful retreat from the city buzz. Key attractions include the stunning Bellevue Beach, the scenic Charlottenlund Forest, and the historic Bakken amusement park. These areas provide a perfect blend of nature, luxury, and tranquillity.

# PRACTICAL INFO

# TRAVEL

Exploring Copenhagen on foot is one of the best ways to absorb the city's charm and beauty. Many of the main attractions, such as Tivoli Gardens, Nyhavn, and Amalienborg Palace, are within walking distance of each other.

Copenhagen is renowned for its cycling culture: it has been named Europe's best biking city multiple years in a row. Cycling offers a unique perspective of the city. Common etiquette includes cycling on the right, raising your hand or fist to signal stopping or slowing down, and indicating turning by sticking out your arm in that direction. Helmets are optional. There are countless shops that rent bikes for a day, or you could download the Donkey Republic bike-sharing app to easily find an orange bike to pick up.

The public transport system is extensive and reliable. You can download the DOT Tickets app to pay for your fares and plan your journeys. It allows you to purchase a City Pass, giving you access to all forms of public transport for 24 hours to 5 days. Alternatively, you can find DOT ticket machines at any station. The metro is in service 24/7. Wait times are never more than 2-4 minutes during rush hour and even in the evening, metros run every 15-20 minutes. There are three lines that overlap at a few stations, so transferring is easy. In 2019, seventeen new stations were added to the metro system. This M3 metro line, also known as the City Circle Line, connects Vesterbro, Frederiksberg, Norrebro, Osterbro, København K. Another great way to get around the city is the Harbour Bus.

DOT

These yellow ferries take you up and down the harbour on a regular bus ticket. The route will take you between places such as The Royal Library, the Opera, Islands Brygge, and Refshaleøen.

Københavns Lufthavne Kastrup or Copenhagen Airport, is located just 8 kilometres south of the city centre. Both the metro and regional trains offer quick and convenient connections to any part of the city. You can take the metro directly from terminal 3 to Kongens Nytorv in only 13 minutes. From Kongens Nytorv you can switch to the M3 metro line. The regional train from the airport to the central station takes 15 minutes. Of course, you could take a taxi into the city, but this will set you back 350-450 DKK.

OTEL CABINN
BLOOM 24.–26. MAJ
ANISH KAPOOR UNSEEN 11.04.24 - 20.10.24
ARKEN

# WHERE TO STAY

**Copenhagen Downtown Hostel**

*Vandkunsten 5, 1467 København K, copenhagendowntown.com*

Situated in the heart of the city, this hostel is the perfect spot for those looking to explore Copenhagen's vibrant nightlife and cultural attractions. The hostel has a lively bar, shared areas for socialising, a variety of room options and reasonable prices.

**Generator Copenhagen**

*Adelgade 5, 7, 1304 København K, staygenerator.com*

Generator is a worldwide hostel chain known for its reliable and affordable accommodation. This centrally located hostel offers both private rooms and dormitory beds, along with a vibrant social atmosphere. Guests can enjoy the on-site bar, café, and regular events, making it a fun place to meet fellow travellers.

**Hotel Christian IV**

*Dronningens Tværgade 45, 1302 København K, hotelchristianiv.dk*

This charming three-star family-owned hotel is centrally located in Indre By. Here you can enjoy a good night's sleep and start the day in the bright breakfast room. After exploring the city, return for a complimentary coffee or tea and pastries in the lounge. Situated on a quiet street near the harbour and Nyhavn, the hotel provides easy access to many restaurants and bars. Room amenities include cable TV, soundproofed windows, and free Wi-Fi.

**Wakeup Copenhagen**

*Borgergade 9, 1300 København K, wakeupcopenhagen.dk*

Are you a budget-conscious traveller? Look no further! With locations near the city centre and waterfront, this hotel offers modern, compact rooms with all the essentials. It's known for its clean and stylish design, providing great value for money without compromising on comfort.

**Urban House Hostel**

*Colbjørnsensgade 5, 11, 1652 København V, meininger-hotels.com*

Urban House Hostel by Meininger is located right next to Copenhagen Central Station. It offers great value for either private rooms with ensuites or dorms with shared facilities. It provides a range of amenities including a guest kitchen, game zone, and bike rental services. It's a fantastic option for families, groups, and solo travellers alike.

**Annex Copenhagen**

*Helgolandsgade 15-17, 1653 København V, annexcopenhagen.dk*

Annex Copenhagen is a trendy family-run hostel in Vesterbro, near Copenhagen Central Station. It offers colourful, comfortable rooms with shared or private bathrooms. Guests can use the amenities at Annex's more luxurious sister Absalon Hotel, including a lounge and a courtyard. Its central location provides easy access to Tivoli Gardens, the Meatpacking District, and various dining options.

HOT
STUFF
DUDE!!

**Steel House Copenhagen**

*Herholdtsgade 6, 1605 København V, steelhousecopenhagen.com*

Affordable accommodation in the heart of Copenhagen, close to Tivoli Gardens and Strøget. In modern Scandinavian décor, it features a range of rooms, from private to dormitories. Guests enjoy free Wi-Fi, a guest kitchen, and a lovely common area. The on-site café serves a breakfast buffet, and bike rentals for exploring the city are available too.

**A&O Copenhagen**

*aoshostels.com*

With the looks of a hotel, this is a stylish and modern hostel offering a touch of luxury at budget prices. Located close to Tivoli Gardens, it features a range of amenities including a pool, gym, and cinema room. The industrial-chic design and atmospheric common areas make it a comfortable and trendy choice for travellers. At A&O, you'll find a variety of affordable room types, from shared dorms to private family rooms. This is a great choice if you want to stay in Nørrebro, one of the city's most diverse areas, popular amongst students and artists. This hostel provides clean and basic facilities at a convenient location with easy access to public transport. There is a second location in Sydhavn.

HOLBÆK
62 KM
KALLUND
BORG 102 KM
JYDERUP
80 KM

# GOOD TO KNOW

### Money

The official currency of Denmark is the Danish krone (DKK). Cash is rarely used anymore in Copenhagen: credit and debit cards are widely accepted. To pay for public transport or rent a bike, you use a phone app or again, your card.

### Language

Most Danes speak excellent English, making it easy to communicate. You'll have no trouble asking for directions or ordering in restaurants. But it's always useful to know a few words, and you can show respect by using *tak*, which means 'thank you', or even *tusind tak*, which literally translates to 'a thousand thanks'. When you're leaving a shop or want to say bye to someone, use *hej hej*; not to be confused with the singular *hej*, which means 'hello'.

### Tipping

Service charges are included in the bill, so tipping in restaurants is not customary. Leaving a small tip for excellent service is always appreciated.

### Dining Hours

Danes normally have their dinner early, with most restaurants opening around 6pm. Reservations are recommended, especially for popular spots.

### Hygge

Embrace *hygge*, the Danish concept of cosiness and

comfort that permeates daily life in Copenhagen. *Hygge* is all about creating a warm and inviting atmosphere that fosters relaxation and connection, whether you're alone with a good book or sharing a meal with friends. You'll find numerous cafés and restaurants that embody this delightful concept. These spaces are designed with soft lighting, comfortable seating, and inviting interiors that make you feel at home from the moment you walk in. Whether it's a chilly winter evening or a sunny summer afternoon, they offer the perfect setting to unwind and enjoy life's simple pleasures.

### Children

Don't be alarmed if you see a child left in their pram on the pavement. This is very common practice in Denmark, where parents will leave their children outside, no matter the weather, so that they can have a little nap and reap the benefits of fresh air.

### Shopping

Shops in Copenhagen generally open around 10am and close by 6pm on weekdays, with shorter hours on weekends. Popular shopping areas include Strøget, one of the longest pedestrian streets in Europe, and trendy neighbourhoods like Nørrebro and Vesterbro for unique boutiques.

### Copenhagen Card

If you plan on visiting a lot of attractions, consider the Copenhagen Card, which offers free entry to over eighty attractions and unlimited use of public transport. It's a great way to save money while seeing the city's top sights. More info on *copenhagencard.com.*

### Weather

Copenhagen's weather can be unpredictable. It's wise to carry an umbrella or a raincoat, as rain is frequent, averaging every other

J. ALTHÉN'S
SKRÄDDERI - AFFÄR
Östergatan 12
GRAND RESTAURANT HIPPODROMEN
NYTT. ELEGANT. FÖRSTKLASSIGT.
COGNAC
GUST. WOLKE
VIN- &
SPIRITUOSA AFFÄR
WOLKES CALORIC
BOUTELLEAU COGNAC
CHRISTENSON & Co.
SKYLTFABRIK
DJEKNEGATAN 4
TELEFON 1307
ANNONSERA GENOM GUMÆLII ANNONSBYRÅ
KÖP
ELMQVIST'S
HANDSKAR
SKOMAKAREGATAN 16
REIJMYRE
GLAS
ÄR FINAST
Ö HAMNGATAN 2 MALMÖ
MALMÖ BILLIGASTE
MANUFAKTUR-&
KAPP-AFFÄR
Florentin Steneberg
HÖRNET AF SÖDER- &
SKOMAKAREGATORNA
ÉTAGE
KFC
APOTEKET

day. Copenhagen can suddenly get very cold as well, so make sure to layer up. Danes have mastered the art of embracing the harsh Nordic winters, which is why you might come across people participating in *Vinterbadning* (winter bathing) in the harbour or sea. People will dip into the freezing waters for good health and rejuvenation.

**Safety**

Copenhagen is generally safe, but like in any urban area, it's wise to stay aware of your surroundings, especially in crowded areas. Keep your belongings secure and be cautious at night.

**Local etiquette**

Danes value personal space and politeness. When entering shops or public transport, greet people with a friendly *hej* (hello). Also, remember to queue patiently and allow others to exit before you board public transport. Danes are known for their punctuality. If you have plans or made a reservation, please arrive on time. Danes might say it's okay when you show up late, but it is quite rude to be more than 15 minutes late.

**Picnic amongst the graves**

In summer, the Danes like to take their picnics to their cemeteries, like Assistens Kirkegård in Nørrebro. This is completely legal, so spread out your blanket and open a can of beer if you want to blend in with the locals. Make sure to stick to the areas with the old graves, though; they will be clearly indicated on the signs. Biking or jogging in cemeteries is common practice as well; no one bats an eye if you stick to the main lanes.

# WHEN TO TRAVEL

# COPENHAGEN IN SPRING

In spring, the days get longer, and the gloomy Danish winter is slowly starting to come to an end. However, you might still get the occasional snowfall at the end of March, or sometimes even in April. As temperatures begin to rise and daylight extends, the city comes to life with colourful flowers and lively events.

The cherry blossoms typically bloom in April, turning some parks into seas of pink. There are a few spots to view the blossom, all of which are free. Bispebjerg Cemetery, in Nordvest, has the most popular collection of cherry blossoms. It can get very busy, with hundreds of people queuing to take pictures. Make sure to go early to avoid the bulk of the crowds. While you're there, make sure to visit Grundtvigs Kirke, a rare example of expressionist church architecture.

The annual Sakura Festival, in Langelinie Park, is usually held at the end of April. This festival is a display of Japanese culture with drum shows, martial arts, and various workshops. Other than that, it is an especially gorgeous place to see the cherry blossoms as it is near the water. If you take a boat tour, which is a great spring activity anyway, you can get a view of them from the water. The Botanical Gardens are gorgeous too, regardless of the season, but here you see the flowers blooming in more spacious surroundings, as the trees are more widely spread.

# COPENHAGEN IN SUMMER

Summer is the best time to visit Copenhagen. The days are super long and there are numerous outdoor places to enjoy a meal and a swim. It is also the perfect season for taking a long stroll along the Copenhagen lakes or going for a boat ride. Have a picnic in Kongeshave, Frederiksberg Garden or Faelledparken. Try the Danish summer favourite *Koldskål*, a cold, sour buttermilk soup you can find in any supermarket. Some people add biscuits, *kammerjunkere*, or just enjoy it as is.

Go swimming at harbour bath Islands Brygge to jump off the structures or go to Sandkaj or Amager Beach Park. Another lovely swimming spot is at La Banchina, where the locals gather to enjoy some wine by the water. Refshaleøen, once home to the world's largest shyipyards, is now a sustainable neighbourhood with a food market, and all sorts of activities to partake in, perfect for a summer's day. Or go sustainable skiing at the green CopenHill. Summer is also festival time. Experience Copenhagen Jazz festival or Distortion, two big events taking place in the great outdoors.

A real Danish summer tradition is Sankt Hans Aften, which is celebrated on the 23rd of June. The summer solstice is tied to the feast of Saint John the Baptist (known in Danish as Sankt Hans). The evening is celebrated with a bonfire, which is to commemorate the witch burning of the 16th and 17th centuries. There are a lot of locations to take part in Sankt Hans Aften traditions and celebrations. Go to Nyhavn, Tivoli Gardens, Ofelia Plads, or Toldboden for some of the most popular watching spots.

# COPENHAGEN IN AUTUMN

In autumn, the city tends to get a little less crowded, and the comforting concept of *hygge* is fully embraced by both locals and visitors. Dress up warm and go for a leisurely walk before having a coffee at one of the city's many cosy cafés. The autumn foliage is simply gorgeous, transforming the city into a sea of reds, oranges, and earthy colours.

Other than the many picturesque lakes and parks, a particularly lovely place for a stroll is Assistens Kirkegård. The historic cemetery, which is the final resting place of Hans Christian Andersen and Søren Kierkegaard among others, is also a great spot to walk the length of the tree-lined paths. On Nørrebrogade and Jagtvej, you'll find numerous inviting cafés where you can take a break from your walk and enjoy a hot drink.

The more frequent wet and windy days make this the perfect season to explore some of the city's world-class museums. Tivoli Gardens is a fantastic place to visit this time of year. Every year, from the beginning of October to early November, Tivoli Gardens is fully dressed up for Halloween, featuring all sorts of events that capture the spirit of the season.

# COPENHAGEN IN WINTER

Winters in Scandinavia can get gloomy quite quickly. Luckily, Copenhagen has many spots to beat the winter blues. The buildings in Copenhagen become illuminated as soon as the sun sets, and there is a whole range of outdoor decorations you can go and see on your winter stroll. Hotel d'Angleterre, the most high-end hotel in Copenhagen, pulls out all the stops when it comes to Christmas decorations. Around mid-November each year, the hotel unveils a new, extravagant façade with lights and decorations. Opposite the hotel, you can visit the Christmas market on Kongens Nytorv. There is another lovely Christmas market at Højbro Plads, which is smaller and a little quainter.

Another festive winter activity is ice skating. There are multiple rinks around the city, but the Broens Ice Rink, located in the heart of the city, is the one with the best views over the harbour. Whilst you wander through the city you may encounter some rather joyous and rowdy Danes. They are probably partaking in a *Julefrokost*. Friends, family or even work colleagues will organise this event to get everyone together at Christmas time to eat *flæskesteg* (roast pork) and wash it down with some *aquavit* (snaps). If you happen to be in Copenhagen during *Fastelavn*, a carnival tradition around February/March, you must dive into one of the cafés to grab some *fastelavnsboller*. This typical snack is made from puff pastry and filled with whipped cream.

LIFE IN
COPENHAGEN

# HISTORY

### Viking village

The earliest records of Copenhagen date back to the 10th century when it was a small Viking fishing village. It was known as Havn, meaning harbour. Eventually Copenhagen became a hub for trading, attracting merchants from across the region. The strategic location along the natural harbour and the Øresund strait, made it an ideal location for fishing as well as trade. The first written reference to Copenhagen was when it was mentioned in a document by King Valdemar the Great as Køpmannæhafn (indeed, with an f), which translates to 'merchants' harbour'.

### Absalon

Copenhagen's growth began in earnest in the 12th century, largely thanks to Bishop Absalon's influence. Absalon, who also served as King Valdemar I's advisor, was granted the village of Havn in 1167. Recognising its strategic importance, Absalon fortified the area by building a castle on the small island of Slotsholmen, which would serve as the foundation for Copenhagen's development. Under Absalon's leadership, Copenhagen began to thrive as a commercial and trading centre. The construction of fortifications and the establishment of the Church of Our Lady (Vor Frue Kirke) contributed to Copenhagen's status as an emerging city. By the late 12th century, it was recognised as a significant urban centre in Denmark.
The harbour was a lot wider than it is today, and one of its

most important bridges is the Børsbroen. This bridge was strategically placed in the 17th century between two of the most influential buildings: Børsen, the old stock exchange, and Christiansborg Palace. This palace, named after Christian IV of Denmark, still marks some of Copenhagen's grandest developments.

#### Christian IV

Following his coronation in 1596, Christian IV of Denmark significantly expanded the town by incorporating new city districts and modern fortifications such as earthworks and bastions. The king commissioned German and Dutch architects and craftsmen to build magnificent structures to boost his prestige. Copenhagen had become Denmark's primary fortified city and naval port by the time Christian IV died in 1648, and the town served as a framework for the Danish kingdom's administration as well as a centre of trade in Northern Europe.

#### Kalmar Union

The Kalmar Union (1397-1523) was a major political alliance in Scandinavia that attempted to unite the kingdoms of Denmark, Norway, and Sweden under a single monarch. The hope was to strengthen their political and economic influence in Europe. Queen Margrete I of Denmark played a key role in the union's formation. She became regent of Denmark in 1375, Norway in 1380, and Sweden in 1389, effectively ruling all three kingdoms. The Union faced significant challenges. Sweden and Norway were unhappy with the Danish domination, because of their loss of autonomy. There were clashes over trade policies and resource allocation. The most

significant challenge came from Sweden, where a series of uprisings and rebellions took place. The Swedish War of Liberation (1521-1523), led by Gustav Vasa, dealt the Kalmar Union a crushing defeat. Following a successful rebellion, Gustav was elected King of Sweden in 1523, effectively ending Swedish participation in the union. The Kalmar Union is generally remembered as an ambitious but ultimately unsuccessful attempt at Nordic unity. Its history continues to be studied and reflected on, highlighting the Scandinavian countries' enduring connections and shared history.

#### Occupation

World War II had a significant impact on Copenhagen. Nazi Germany invaded Denmark in April 1940, occupying Copenhagen along with the rest of the country. The Danish government chose to cooperate with the occupiers to avoid widespread destruction, resulting in a relatively mild occupation compared to other European countries. During the Nazi presence, Copenhagen became a hub of resistance activity. Danish resistance fighters sabotaged German installations and helped Danish Jews escape to neutral Sweden. In 1943, the Danish government resigned, and German authorities declared martial law. This resulted in increased resistance and major confrontations with the occupiers. As part of the resistance, many Danish naval ships were sunk in the Copenhagen harbour to prevent them from being used by the Germans. Copenhagen was liberated in May 1945, following the German surrender.

#### Urban planning

In the latter half of the

20th century, Copenhagen underwent significant transformations, making it well-known for its urban planning, quality of life and sustainability. The Øresund toll bridge connects Copenhagen and Malmö for both road and rail traffic. Carl XVI Gustaf of Sweden and Margrethe II of Denmark inaugurated it in July 2000. The bridge now brings Sweden and Denmark even closer, easing travel for commuters and visitors alike. Consequently, Copenhagen has developed into the hub of a wider metropolitan region that includes both countries. The public transport network has undergone major modifications since the bridge's construction, and Amager, south of København K, has undergone extensive reconstruction.

### Greenland

Although Denmark is a small country with a population of around 5.9 million, the Danish kingdom encompasses the islands of Greenland and Bornholm too. Greenland, the world's largest island, is a territory within the Kingdom of Denmark. Its history is intricately linked to both Inuit culture and European exploration. It has been inhabited by Arctic peoples for at least 4,500 years, and their descendants include today's Inuit population. The first Europeans to reach Greenland were Norse settlers from Iceland, led by Erik the Red in 985 CE. These settlements, primarily in the south, existed for several centuries before disappearing in the 15th century, likely because of climate change and isolation. Denmark-Norway resumed contact with Greenland in the early 18th century. In 1721, Danish missionary Hans Egede established a mission in Nuuk, Greenland's current capital. Over the centuries, Greenland gradually became more

↓ GREENLAND

↓ CIRKELBROEN BY OLAFUR ELIASSON

integrated with Denmark, while maintaining a significant degree of cultural and social autonomy. It was granted home rule in 1979 and additional autonomy in 2009, allowing Greenland to manage most of its domestic affairs while Denmark handles foreign policy and defence. The island's economy is primarily based on fishing and hunting, but tourism and mining are becoming increasingly important.

### Bornholm

Bornholm, an island in the Baltic Sea, has a rich history, distinguished by its strategic location and cultural exchanges. Archaeological evidence suggests that it has been inhabited since the Palaeolithic period. Bornholm has had many rulers over the centuries, including Danes, Swedes, Germans, and even the Hanseatic League. Bornholm was a major trade and crafts centre during the Middle Ages, with churches and fortresses to its credit. The island was part of Denmark's crown, but its strategic location made it a frequent target of other powers. Today, Bornholm is known for its tourism, attracting visitors because of its picturesque landscapes and historical sites.

### Danish Design

Danish design is internationally renowned for its simplicity, functionality, and timeless elegance. It started in the 20th century and was influenced by the German Bauhaus School. The design is based on principles of minimalism, emphasising clean lines, high-quality materials, and a seamless integration of form and function. Iconic Danish designers such as Arne Jacobsen (he designed his famous Egg Chair in 1959) and Hans Wegner (who created chairs for the Fritz Hansen company and is known for his The Wishbone Chair, 1949) have created furniture and home accessories that combine attractiveness and functionality. Danish design has influenced architecture, fashion, and everyday objects, embodying the philosophy that beauty and utility should coexist peacefully.

### Sustainability and quality of life

Denmark is a world leader in sustainable development, urban planning, and quality of life. The country's cities are meticulously planned to encourage green living and

minimise environmental impact. Copenhagen especially is known for its extensive cycling infrastructure, efficient public transport, and green spaces that improve city life. The first bike lane in Copenhagen dates from 1892 and by 1912 there was already 50 km of bike lanes in the city. Nowadays, there is 546 km of bike paths. Danish urban planning prioritises residents' well-being by incorporating sustainable practices such as energy-efficient buildings and renewable energy sources. This commitment to sustainability and thoughtful urban design significantly contributes to the country's high standard of living.

# SIGHTSEEING

**Christiania**

*Bådsmandsstræde 43, 1407 København K, christiania.org*

Christiania is an autonomous neighbourhood that was founded in 1971 when a group of people cut a hole in the fence of the military barracks on Bådsmandsstræde. Eventually, the 'town' became known for its alternative lifestyle, street art, and distinct culture, with many of the original settlers still living there today. Most of the structures were built by the inhabitants themselves, giving the town its interesting architecture. You'll find all sorts of cultural experiences in Christiania, restaurants with a focus on sustainability, galleries, and music venues. The Freetown operates under a pseudo-anarchist consensus democracy, meaning each inhabitant is responsible for the community's overall finances, as well as its business and construction. Christiania was mostly known for its relaxed approach to marijuana and other drugs, which used to be sold openly on 'Pusher Street'. That has been shut down in early 2024 to make way for playgrounds and other community spaces. When the street was dug up, locals were allowed to take home a brick each as a souvenir. Make sure to read the Dos and Don'ts at the entrance gate when you come for a visit.

**Botanisk Have**

*Gothersgade 128, 1123 København K, snm.ku.dk*

An absolute must-visit for nature enthusiasts. The indoor area of the Botanical Gardens is housed in a big glass dome-like structure. The outdoor gardens and Palmehuset (Palm House) are must-sees. The 1874 cast-iron spiral staircase in the Palm House has the best view of the flora. The gardens are part of the University of Copenhagen and feature a vast collection of plants and flowers. The garden was first established in 1600, and it was moved twice before settling permanently at its current location in 1874.

↓ CHRISTIANIA

↓ BOTANISK HAVE

**Copenhagen University Library**

*Fiolstræde 1, 1171 København K*

Founded in 1482, the University Library is the oldest library in Denmark and is located just a stone's throw from the famous Round Tower. After undergoing renovations, it was reopened in the autumn of 2023. The building's Neo-Gothic design gives it a real *Harry Potter* feel and is worth taking a peek if you're in the area.

**Operaparken**

*Ekvipagemestervej 18, 1438 København K, cobe.dk*

In the Opera Park visitors walk among trees, plants and flowers from all over the world, carefully selected for their colour variation throughout the year. The park's flora will change in appearance, scent, colour, and density according to the season and depending on where you are in the park.

**Amalienborg**

*Amalienborg Slotsplads, 1257 København K, kongernessamling.dk*

This palace is the home of one of the world's oldest monarchies. The four identical Rococo buildings each are home to one of the members of the royal family, with a flag outside to indicate if its inhabitant is home. The Palace is also known for its changing of the guard. The royal guard marches daily at 12pm from their barracks by Rosenborg Castle through the streets of Copenhagen, often accompanied by music.

**Marmorkirken**

*Frederiksgade 4, 1265 København K, marmorkirken.dk*

Officially named Frederik's church, this church aligns beautifully with Amalienborg palace and the Opera. The building took over a hundred years to finish due to the architect's death as well as financial troubles. This caused the marble to be changed to limestone blocks. So, despite its name, it is not really made from marble. It was finally finished in 1894, which was 145 years after the first effort to build it. The large green dome (made from copper) is a quintessential Copenhagen sight.

**Vor Fresels Kirke**

*Sankt Annæ Gade 29, 1416 København K, vorfrelserskirke.dk*

The iconic Church of Our Saviour was consecrated in 1696. Its serpentine spire can be seen from all over the city. More than 200,000 people climb the 400 steps to the top of the Baroque building annually. The carillon holds as many as 48 bells.

**Christiansborg Slot**

*Prins Jørgens Gård 1, 1218 København K, kongeligeslotte.dk*

This palace, which currently houses the Danish Parliament, Supreme Court, and Ministry of State, used to be one of the main residential palaces of the Danish royal family. You can visit the Royal reception Rooms and the ruins underneath the palace.

↓ AMALIENBORG

↓ DEN LILLE HAVFRUE

**Rosenborg Slot**

*Øster Voldgade 4A, 1350 København K, kongernessamling.dk*

Originally built in the early 17th century as a summer house for Christian IV. The Castle is part of the King's Garden, a park where the castle serves as a majestic backdrop. You'll also find the Danish crown jewels and other royal treasures.

**Den Lille Havfrue**

*Langelinie, 2100 København Ø*

The Little Mermaid statue by Edvard Eriksen, *Den Lille Havfrue*, is one of Copenhagen's most visited landmarks, often being used in promotional material as an iconic part of the city. It was a gift from Danish brewer Carl Jacobsen to the City of Copenhagen and was unveiled in 1913. It is one of the most visited sights, but also one of the smallest. In fact, many are underwhelmed by the Little Mermaid due to its size and the crowds.

**Kastellet**

*Gl. Hovedvagt, Kastellet 1, 2100 København Ø, kastellet.dk*

Close to the Little Mermaid statue you'll find Kastellet. This citadel is one of the best-preserved fortresses in Northern Europe. When it was built in the 1600s, it served as barracks for the military of Copenhagen. During World War II it was occupied by German forces. Today, the buildings inside the citadel are still used for military purposes. The star-shape of Kastellet and its Dutch Renaissance-style architecture are the perfect backdrop for a leisurely stroll. You will come across many locals going for a run or a walk by the water.

**Superkilen**

*Nørrebrogade 210,
2200 København N,
visitcopenhagen.com*

Right in the heart of Nørrebro, you'll find this urban space designed by Bjarke Ingels Group, Superflex, and Topetek1. It's a celebration of cultural diversity, featuring three colour-coded zones (red, black, and green) filled with objects from over sixty countries (lampposts, benches, waste bins, from all over Europe), reflecting the neighbourhood's multicultural spirit. Most photographed: the black hill with wobbly white lines (see page 34), which is part of the skate park.

↓ BOTANISK HAVE

↓ SUPERKILEN

HERRENS ORD BLIVER EVINDELIG

# MUSEUMS

Most museums offer student discounts and free admission once a month, so check their websites for updates and ticket sales. Additionally, you can get a Parkmuseerne ticket, which gives you access to the six museums situated in Copenhagen's green museum district, which includes the Statens Museum for Kunst and Rosenborg Castle (*parkmuseerne.dk*).

**Copenhagen Contemporary**

*Refshalevej 173A, 1432 København K, copenhagencontemporary.org*

This international contemporary art centre exhibits installation art from around the world. It is located on Refshaleøen and offers 7,000 square metres of beautiful industrial space for artworks of large formats that trigger all the senses.

**Designmuseum Danmark**

*Bredgade 68, 1260 København K, designmuseum.dk*

Explore the unique qualities of Danish design in furniture, fashion, posters, and ceramics at this remarkable museum housed in a 18th-century Rococo building. Highlights include a permanent exhibition of Danish chairs, featuring important designs by designers such as Hans Wegner and Arne Jacobsen. It also focuses on contemporary Danish design, examining the nation's influence on product design, graphic design, and design for public spaces. They put on fascinating temporary exhibitions too.

↓ NY CARLSBERG GLYPTOTEK

↓ PLANETARIUM

↓ NY CARLSBERG GLYPTOTEK

↓ STATENS MUSEUM FOR KUNST

**Dansk Arkitektur Center**

*Bryghusgade 10, 1473 København K, dac.dk*

The Danish Architecture Center (DAC) is a must-visit international cultural attraction located on Copenhagen's harbourside. Exhibitions at DAC are regularly updated and showcase the latest architectural trends, as well as insights from leading Danish architects. The permanent exhibition tells the story of Danish architecture from the Viking Age to the present, and you will learn how Danish architecture is fundamental to Danish cultural understanding, and how it plays a central role in life. You can also book a tour with a personal guide, who will give you an up-close experience of the museum. The DAC Café offers three rooftop terraces for drinks and dinner, giving you a unique view of the city.

**Lykkemuseet**

*Admiralgade 19, 1066 København K, thehappinessmuseum.com*

*Lykke* means happiness in Danish, and that is exactly what this museum is all about. It's small, and it will take you just 30-45 minutes to get through it. The focus of the museum is on happiness: where it comes from, how you measure it, why Denmark has often been named the happiest country on earth, and, of course, the concept of *hygge* and its relation to happiness. The museum was created by the Happiness Research Institute, a think tank focusing on wellbeing, happiness, and quality of life.

**Nationalmuseet**

*Ny Vestergade 10, 1471 København K, natmus.dk*

Visit the largest museum in Denmark to learn about the history of the nation from prehistoric times to the present. The Inuit and Viking exhibits are captivating, and the Trundholm Sun Chariot, a magnificent Bronze Age relic discovered by a farmer in 1902, is one of the prehistoric highlights. Another is the so-called Egtved Girl's grave, which houses the remarkably preserved body of a woman buried nearly 3,500 years ago. The thought-provoking and interesting exhibitions on Denmark's colonial past in the Caribbean, India, West Africa, and Greenland, are a must-see.

**Statens Museum for Kunst (SMK)**

*Sølvgade 48-50, 1307 København K, smk.dk*

The National Gallery of Denmark houses the country's largest collection of art, and even the building itself is an artwork. Featuring an extensive collection of European and Danish art spanning from the 14th century to the present, the museum continues to be the primary cultural hub of the city. It is nearly impossible to see everything in a single day, so make your selections wisely. Highlights include the subdued interiors of Vilhelm Hammershøi's 19th-century Copenhagen and the exquisitely lit landscapes of the Skagen School. Keep an eye out for SMK Fridays, when the museum opens late, admission is free, and a variety of events are hosted, including street food, drinks, and live music.

**Københavns Museum**

*Stormgade 18, 1555 København V, cphmuseum.kk.dk*

The Museum of Copenhagen is a must for history and city lovers. This is the official museum of Copenhagen, documenting the city's history from the 12th century to now. It was established in 1891 and is built in Neoclassical style. It has interesting and well-structured explanations of the city's history through diverse media, and admission is free on the last Wednesday of each month. The museum operates in affiliation with the Thorvaldsen Museum and Kunsthallen Nikolaj.

**Ny Carlsberg Glyptotek**

*Dantes Plads 7, 1556 København V, glyptoteket.com*

The Glyptotek was founded in 1888 by brewing tycoon Carl Jacobsen as a public gallery for his personal art collection. Today, it is home to an exceptional collection that includes sculptures from ancient Egypt, Rome, and Greece, paintings from the Danish Golden Age, and an amazing assortment of works by French Impressionists. It is also possible to see the complete series of Degas' bronzes and 35 sculptures by Rodin. The museum's glass-domed Winter Garden, with a fountain, palm trees, and statues, is another highlight. Entrance to the museum is free on Tuesdays.

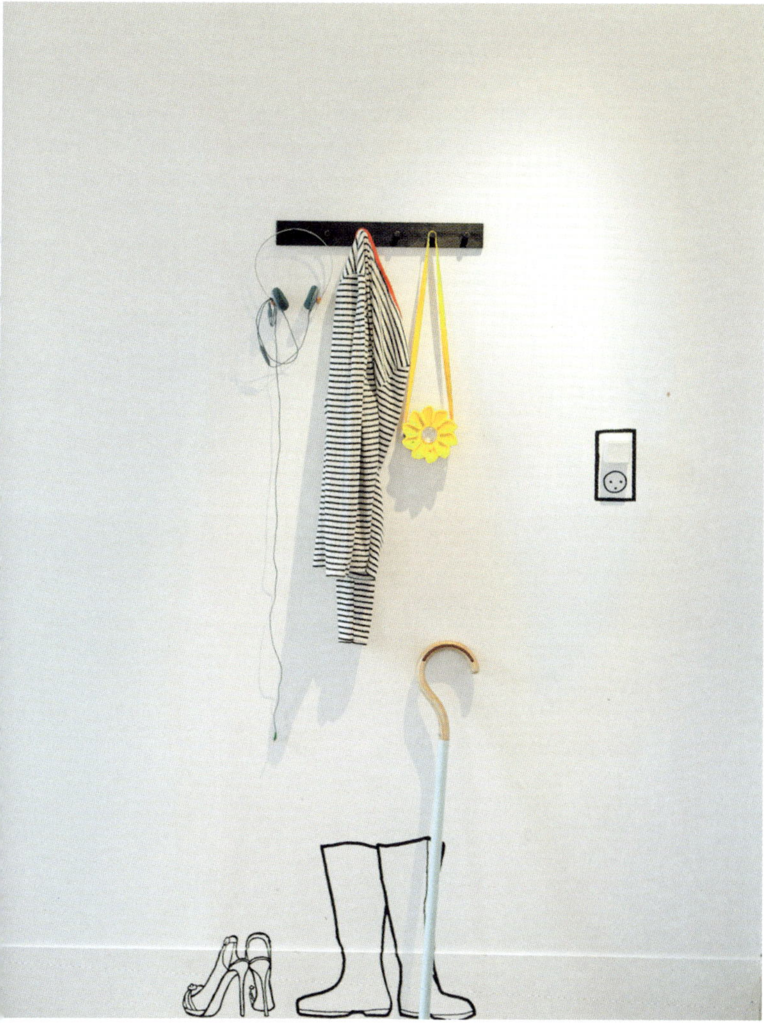

**Planetarium**

*Gammel Kongevej 10,*
*1610 København V,*
*planetarium.dk*

A visit to the Planetarium will take you straight into space and leave you starry-eyed. In the large dome you can truly immerse yourself into the wonders of space, and watch films about volcanoes, astronauts, and space exploration. The dome, the heart of the Planetarium, is the largest in Northern Europe. It offers a unique experience, making you feel fully immersed in the space experience. Most of the films and shows are narrated in Danish, but you can ask for an English headset at the entrance.

↓ PLANETARIUM

↓ NY CARLSBERG GLYPTOTEK

# STREET ART

Copenhagen is famous not only for its historical landmarks and modern architecture, but also for its thriving street-art scene. The city's walls, gables, and public spaces serve as canvases for local and international artists, transforming urban landscapes into vibrant art installations.

**Conor Harrington**

*Tullinsgade 7, 1618 København V, insta @conorsaysboom*

Conor Harrington, an Irish street artist known for his striking large-scale murals, has left his mark on Copenhagen. His artwork on Tullinsgade 7 features his signature blend of classical painting techniques and contemporary urban elements and was created in June 2015 as part of the 'Surface Project'. The Danish photographer Søren Solkær invited six artists, including Conor Harrington, to create murals in Copenhagen for this major exhibition.

**Peter Abelin & Erik Jerichau**

*Halmtorvet 27, 1700 København V*

Walking down Halmtorvet, one of Vesterbro's main streets, you might notice a building with a skylight. On sunny days, you might think you're looking through an archway. This trompe l'oeil was created in 1991 on the back of the offices of Nomeco, a pharmaceutical company. You'll find it close to Art Hub Copenhagen.

**Sortedams Dossering**

*Ryesgade 18, 2200 København N*

Alongside Sortedam Lake, you will find a range of sculptures and other street art. A mural at Ryesgade, spread across a vast wall along the cycling path, depicts a sleeping man and woman. The mural was created by Ulrik Schiødt, who is well-known for his visualisation and conceptualisation of depth and contrast.

**The Open-Air Gable Gallery**

*2400 København NV*

Some of the best street art in Copenhagen can be found in the city's least touristy residential area of Nordvest. Visit the open-air murals located along Møntmestervej and Rentemestervej. This outdoor gallery features works by both emerging and established artists, making it a must-visit for anyone interested in contemporary street art. The murals often reflect social issues, local culture, and artistic experimentation, creating a vibrant and thought-provoking urban gallery. The façades are regularly updated and reflect a wide range of themes from political statements to abstract designs.

**ZUSA**

*fb @anders.thordal.9*

Going *ZUSA* hunting is an activity in itself. The four letters Z-U-S-A, pop up high on the sides of buildings all over Copenhagen. The letters, which stand for *Zusammen*, 'together' in German, are designed and painted by street artist legend Anders Thordal, who has been part of the Copenhagen street art movement since the 1980s. He studied at Denmark Design School before developing MS at the age of 28 and becoming wheelchair dependent. His illness hasn't stifled his creativity, and he is still very active, although reliant on a group of assistants who, once he has created the large letters, erect the artwork for him.

# CINEMA

If the rainy weather in Copenhagen has left you with an urge to go cosy up to watch a film, there are many places to go. Danish cinemas will show English films with Danish subtitles, and often Danish films with English subtitles.

**Cinemateket**

*Gothersgade 55, 1123 København K, dfi.dk*

Cinemateket is housed in the Danish Film Institute's buildings and contains three cinemas named after prominent figures in Danish film history: Carl (Theodor Dreyer), Asta (Nielsen) and Benjamin (Christensen). The first floor also hosts a comprehensive library of film and television literature, with an extensive catalogue of feature films, documentaries, and TV series. You can also immerse yourself in Danish films with English subtitles; check their website for the programme.

**Grand Teatret**

*Mikkel Bryggers Gade 8, 1460 København K, grandteatret.dk*

A small theatre that screens European arthouse films. There are six screens in total, and all films are shown with original soundtracks and Danish subtitles, so make sure to check the original language of the film you want to watch first.

**Palads**

*Axeltorv 9, 1609 København V, nfbio.dk*

One of Copenhagen's most iconic cinemas, known for its colourful and eye-catching exterior. This cinema houses a total of seventeen screens, so there are always plenty of films to choose from. You will see a lot of families at Palads if you happen to go during the day.

**Imperial Bio**

*Ved Vesterport 4, 1612 København V, nfbio.dk*

The largest cinema in Scandinavia, regularly used for film premieres. In 2015, Imperial won the award 'Classic Screen of the Year', highlighting the advancements Imperial has made in cinema technology. Owned by the same company as Palads, Imperial has the same collection of films.

**Empire Bio**

*Guldbergsgade 29F, 2200 København N, empirebio.dk*

Empire Bio, located in trendy Nørrebro, is a beloved arthouse cinema known for its eclectic film selection and cosy atmosphere. The cinema shows both mainstream films and independent, foreign, and Danish films. The auditoriums also feature double-seats, and large chairs with extra legroom, enhancing the film watching experience. Next door, you will find Bæst, a popular Italian restaurant, and BRUS Bar, a trendy brewpub, to enjoy some pizza or a drink before or after.

PALADS
ROBOT DREAMS
KINGDOM
PLANET APES
I BIOGRAFEN FRA
8. MAJ

COPENHAGEN
COOKING

# FESTIVALS

### CPH:DOX

During this ten-day festival, the largest of its kind in Scandinavia, Copenhagen's international documentary film festival presents a programme that ranges from large-scale theatrical releases to smaller documentaries that will not be shown in cinemas or on TV.
*cphdox.dk*

### Copenhagen Beer Week

Copenhagen Beer Week takes place in May, kicking off with the Mikkeller Beer Celebration, revolving around craft beer. You'll find hundreds of beers from all over the world to try. Beer Week concludes with Ølfestival.
*cphbw.dk*

### Copenhagen Carnival

During Whitsun, this celebration of world music takes place in Fælledparken and on various streets around the city. With samba music at its forefront, there are numerous concerts showcasing thousands of dancers.
*karneval-kbh.dk*

### Distortion Street Festival

Distortion, a week-long street festival with all kinds of music and parties, takes place all over Copenhagen in multiple venues around May/June. It is one of Europe's largest annual festivals, attracting an estimated 100,000 guests daily.
*cphdistortion.dk*

### Copenhagen Jazz Festival

The jazz festival takes place in July and has previously hosted legends such as Ray Charles, Herbie Hancock, and Dizzy Gillespie. Every year over 250,000 people attend at least one of the events.
*jazz.dk*

### Aiasound

Aiasound is a three-day music festival that takes place at the beginning of August, featuring a range of both international and Danish artists.
*aiasound.dk*

### Copenhagen Pride

This Pride Festival, the largest in the Nordic countries, takes place in August. The highlight is the pride parade, with more than 250,000 participants and over 300,000 spectators.
*copenhagenpride.dk*

### Copenhagen Cooking Festival

One of the biggest open-air food festivals in Northern Europe. It celebrates Nordic food and takes place in August. You'll find plenty of events in English or not requiring knowledge of the Danish language.
*copenhagencooking.dk*

### Strøm Festival

This festival takes place year-round with multiple events throughout the city, but culminates in August. It focuses on electronic music, with lesser-known artists and DJs performing, giving it a real underground feel.
*strm.dk*

# THINGS TO DO

### beCopenhagen

You'll find bike tours all throughout Copenhagen. At most major bike rental spots, you will find ads for guided tours. Check out beCopenhagen for a variety of bike tours, such as Contemporary Architecture or The Essential Copenhagen Bike Tour.
*becopenhagen.dk*

### Copenhagen Food Tours

These guided walking tours take you past all the best food spots in town, giving insight into Copenhagen's food culture and history. There are various tours available, such as Street Art and Food, or A Culinary Adventure.
*foodtours.eu*

### GoBoat

Take yourself, and up to eight friends, on your own boat tour. GoBoat has many small electric boats that do not require a licence. They are easy to navigate, and the staff will give you thorough instructions. Bring some snacks or drinks and discover the waters of Copenhagen at your own pace.
*goboat.dk*

### Hey Captain

Hey Captain offers guided tours on water. The captains show you all their favourite places and hidden gems in a very relaxed, intimate setting. Take the public tour or book a private one for your captain to customise the trip to your liking.
*heycaptain.dk*

### Green Kayak

Act against pollution and have fun at the same time. Green kayaks are free to use if you

collect waste on the water and share your experience on social media. You can find them on several locations; check their website for details.
*greenkayak.org*

**Kayak Republic**

If you want to be active while exploring Copenhagen from the water, head to Kayak Republic. Rent kayaks or paddle boards and venture onto the canals at your own pace. They also have a great outdoor bar and terrace.
*Børskaj 12, 1221 København K, kayakrepublic.dk*

**Tivoli Gardens**

A real Copenhagen institution. Especially at night, the majestic allure will leave you eager to go in. As one of the oldest theme parks in the world, it inspired legends like Walt Disney and Hans Christian Andersen. Many rides are centred around fairy tales, seamlessly blending into

↓ COPENHILL

↓ TIVOLI GARDENS

the charming surroundings. You can buy an entry pass for 150 DKK or a ride pass for 300 DKK.
*Vesterbrogade 3, 1630 København V, tivoligardens.com*

**Pumpehuset's Byhaven**

In a little green oasis in the middle of the city, you'll find Pumpehuset's outdoor venue and bar Byhaven. In a welcoming atmosphere with fairy lights, parasols, food, drinks, and lots of greenery, lots of free concerts are organised from April to September. Check the website to see what's on.
*Studiestræde 52, 1554 København V, byhavenkbh.dk*

**CopenHill**

This multifaceted location, created by architect Bjarke Ingels, is not only an architectural masterpiece but also a combined heat and power waste-to-energy plant. It features an artificial ski slope, a climbing wall, and a hiking trail. Access to the rooftop and its cafe is free. Skiing or sledding will cost around 350 DKK.
*Vindmøllevej 6, 2300 København S, copenhill.dk*

**Bakken**

The oldest amusement park in the world dates back to 1583 and can be found only ten minutes north of Copenhagen. It is small but offers a thrilling range of activities, including inversion rides, shooting galleries, and gaming arcades. Access to the park itself is free, and you can buy a multiride ticket for 329 DKK.
*Dyrehavsbakken 207, 2930 Klampenborg, bakken.dk*

↓ KAYAK REPUBLIC

# FAMOUS PEOPLE

**Hans Christian Andersen**

One of Denmark's best-known authors, Hans Christian Andersen is most recognised for his fairy tales, which include *The Little Mermaid*, *The Ugly Duckling*, and *Thumbelina*. His tales have been translated into many languages and are still beloved by readers of all ages everywhere. H.C. Andersen spent most of his life living and working in Copenhagen, and his final resting place can be visited at Assistens Kirkegård.

**Niels Bohr**

Niels Bohr, a trailblazing physicist, significantly advanced our knowledge of quantum mechanics and atomic structure. In 1920, he founded the Institute of Theoretical Physics at the University of Copenhagen, which was named after him in 1965. His research on atomic structure earned him the 1922 Nobel Prize in Physics. In the 1930s, he helped refugees flee the Nazis. When his family – considered Jewish by the occupiers – was about to be arrested in 1943, he fled to Sweden and soon after moved to Britain, where he helped in the development of the atomic bomb. After the war, he promoted the peaceful applications of atomic energy.

**Lukas Graham**

The Danish band Lukas Graham, well-known for their soulful pop sound, is named after their lead vocalist. He grew up in Freetown Christiania, about which he often writes in his lyrics. With hits like *7 Years* and *Mama Said*, the band has received multiple nominations and awards for their music, which frequently reflects emotional and personal themes that resonate with listeners around the world.

#### Hamlet

Despite being a fictional character, Hamlet has a strong cultural connection to Denmark because of William Shakespeare's well-known play of the same name. The narrative takes place in the Danish castle of Kronborg, and Hamlet has come to represent themes of tragedy, retribution, and self-examination.

#### Bjarke Ingels

Copenhagen architect Bjarke Ingels has won praise from around the world for his avant-garde designs that frequently include futuristic and sustainable elements. Two stand-out projects are Copenhagen's CopenHill waste-to-energy plant and New York's VIA 57 West.

#### Arne Jacobsen

Copenhagen's own Arne Jacobsen is a true Danish icon. He was a prolific designer and architect whose work has influenced modern design and architecture. Known for his practical and minimalist designs, The Egg Chair and The Swan Chair are recognised around the world. He designed several famous buildings in the Danish capital, such as the SAS Royal Hotel.

#### Søren Kierkegaard

Renowned theologian and philosopher Søren Kierkegaard is frequently referred to as the founder of existentialism. His insightful essays on psychology, religion, and ethics have influenced modern philosophy and thought for a very long time. He loved walking through his hometown, and famously said: "Some of my fellow countrymen no doubt think that Copenhagen is a boring little town. But I think (...) it's the greatest place I could ask for. Big enough to be a fair-sized city, small enough that there isn't a price tag on people."

**Queen Margrethe II**

From 1972, Margrethe II ruled Denmark as its monarch. She is well-known for her creative abilities and artistic contributions, often producing eclectic, colourful, and stylish pieces.  She worked as a production and costume designer, participated in archaeological excavations, co-wrote film scripts, and as a crown princess illustrated *Lord of the Rings*. Margrethe is often nicknamed 'the Ashtray Queen', being an unrepentant chain smoker. During her reign, the monarchy underwent significant modernisation, and she is still a beloved and esteemed figure in Danish society. She announced her abdication during her New Year's Eve address to the nation in 2023, and left the throne after exactly 52 years, on 14th January 2024.

**Mads Mikkelsen**

Østerbro-born actor Mads Mikkelsen is well-known for his adaptable roles in both Hollywood and European motion pictures. His performances in *Casino Royale*, *Doctor Strange*, *The Hunt*, and the television series *Hannibal* brought him recognition on a global scale. Mikkelsen has established himself as one of the greatest actors of his generation with his captivating performances and unique presence.

**Holger Rune**

In the tennis world, Holger Rune is one of the rising stars. His impressive performances and commitment to the sport have helped him establish himself as one of Denmark's most promising young athletes on the international tennis circuit.

### Josephine Skriver

Famous Danish model Josephine Skriver is well-known for her collaborations with high-end fashion labels like Gucci, Dolce & Gabbana, and Victoria's Secret. Born in Copenhagen to a gay father and lesbian mother, she uses her platform to advocate for equality and acceptance and is a vocal supporter of LGBTQ+ rights.

NYHAVN 17

FREDSFONDENS HUS
CAP HORN

# FILMS & SERIES IN AND ABOUT DENMARK

**The Danish Girl (2015)**

*The Danish Girl* is a biographical drama by Tom Hooper, about the lives of Danish artists Lili Elbe and Gerda Wegener. The film is based on David Ebershoff's 2000 novel and features renowned actors such as Eddie Redmayne and Alicia Vikander. The film does a fantastic job of capturing Copenhagen in the early 20th century; scenes are shot at famous locations like Nyhavn and the Royal Danish Theatre. The moving tale of Lili Elbe, one of the first known patients of gender reassignment surgery, is enhanced by the film's portrayal of the city.

**Copenhagen (2014)**

Mark Raso's coming-of-age film tells the tale of a Canadian man (Gethin Anthony) who visits Copenhagen in search of his grandfather's past. He befriends a waitress (Frederikke Dahl Hansen) who agrees to serve as his translator and guide. Amid the breathtaking backdrop of Copenhagen, the film offers a poignant examination of relationships and self-discovery as it guides viewers through the city's charming streets and canals.

**Festen (The Celebration, 1998)**

This film, directed by Thomas Vinterberg, tells the story of a businessman celebrating his birthday with his family and town dignitaries. During the course of the party, however, many dark secrets about the family's past are revealed. *Festen* celebrates naturalistic and minimalist filmmaking as part of the Danish Dogme 95 movement, a set of rules also referred to as 'The Vow of Chastity'. Dogme 95 productions aimed to create films free from the artifice of Hollywood, aiming to be more genuine. Skjoldenæsholm Castle, a fifty-minute drive from Copenhagen, was the filming location.

**En kongelig affære**
**(A Royal Affair, 2012)**

This story is set in the 18th century, at the court of the mentally ill King Christian VII of Denmark and his Queen Caroline Matilda. She secretly falls in love with her German physician, Johann Friedrich von Struensee, and together they start a revolution. With famous actors such as Danish Mads Mikkelsen and Swedish Alicia Vikander, the film was filmed mostly in the Czech Republic, but still captures the ins and outs of the Danish King's court.

**Druk (Another Round, 2020)**

Thomas Vinterberg directed the film *Druk*, or 'binge drinking'. The film follows four teachers who lose interest in their profession as they struggle with unmotivated students, and their lives seem boring and stale. The group eventually discusses a theory by psychiatrist Finn Skårderud, that humans have a blood alcohol level that is 0.05 per cent too low. The friends embark on an experiment to test the theory. The story is raw and tells a tale of life. *Druk* was dedicated to Vinterberg's daughter Ida, who tragically passed away in a car crash four days after filming started. The script was then rewritten to become about awakening to life. Ida provided inspiration for the film, telling stories of student drinking culture, including scenes with real high-school graduates, depicting various graduation and drinking traditions.

### The Little Mermaid (2023)

Although Disney's *Little Mermaid* has little connection to Denmark, it is still loosely based on Hans Christian Andersen's original story. With colourful characters and upbeat songs, Disney's rendition leaves out some of Andersen's more gruesome themes, like the original mermaid dissolving into sea foam. But why have all that drama when you can have a talking crab singing Calypso tunes?

### A Beautiful Life (2023)

Danish musical drama *A Beautiful Life* narrates the story of Elliott, a young fisherman who has a secret gift for singing. When renowned music manager Suzanne finds him, his life takes an unexpected turn because she recognises potential in his undeveloped talent. Elliott must deal with the pressures of his sudden prominence while staying true to his roots as he finds himself in the public eye. The story takes a transformative turn from the poor fishing village where Elliott grew up to the wealthy upscale life of the music manager. Elliott is portrayed by famous Danish singer Christopher, who subsequently went on a world tour singing the songs featured in the film. Scenes are filmed in various parts of Denmark, including at the Round Tower in Copenhagen.

### Broen (The Bridge, 2011-2018)

Under the Danish and Swedish titles *Broen* and *Bron* respectively, this thrilling popular crime series and joint Danish-Swedish production, begins on the Øresund Bridge, which connects Copenhagen with Malmö (Sweden). The discovery of a dead body in the middle of the bridge calls for a joint investigation. Danish and Swedish police detectives must work together to uncover the makings of the crime. This film also highlights the cultural and geographical connections between Denmark and Sweden, making it an especially interesting watch.

**The Rain (2018-2020)**

*The Rain* is a post-apocalyptic Danish series that picks up six years after a vicious virus, spread by rain, kills almost the whole human population in Scandinavia. After emerging from a bunker, siblings Simone (Alba August) and Rasmus (Lucas Lynggaard Tønnesen) discover a drastically altered world. They join other survivors navigating the dangers and difficulties of this new reality as they look for their father, who might hold the key to a cure. The series gives a unique take on the post-apocalyptic genre, taking place in Denmark and Sweden. It featured scenes at the theme park Bakken, painting it in a very different post-apocalyptic light compared to the joyous theme park it is now.

**Borgen (2010-2022)**

The highly regarded political drama *Borgen*, written by Adam Price, provides a detailed examination of the inner workings of Danish politics. The show focuses on fictional character Birgitte Nyborg, the first female prime minister of Denmark, and explores the difficulties she has in juggling her personal and professional lives and her rise to power. Filmed in and around Copenhagen, *Borgen* offers an engrossing depiction of Danish politics. The series is set in Christiansborg, the palace that houses the Danish parliament.

# BOOKS IN & ABOUT DENMARK

**The Copenhagen Trilogy – Tove Ditlevsen**

This autobiographical trilogy tells the story of one woman's journey from a troubled girlhood in working-class Copenhagen through her struggle to live on her own terms. Ditlevsen's profound and personal memoir tells the story of her life in Copenhagen from childhood to adulthood. The trilogy – *Childhood*, *Youth*, and *Dependency* – provides a candid and unvarnished depiction of her battles with addiction, love, and identity. Her vivid writing conveys a very intimate perspective on Copenhagen, encapsulating the spirit of the city's streets and people.

**Out of Africa – Karen Blixen**

Karen Blixen, better known by her pen name Isak Dinesen, is one of Denmark's most widely acclaimed modern authors. Although the story is mostly set in Kenya, the memoir recounts the events of Blixen's move to British East Africa in late 1913 to marry her second cousin and make a life by running a coffee plantation on the slopes of Mount Kilimanjaro.

**Number the Stars – Lois Lowry**

This piece of historical fiction tells the story of a young Danish girl during World War II. Set in Copenhagen, the book explores themes of bravery, friendship, and resistance as the girl, Annemarie, helps her Jewish friend escape the Nazis.

**Copenhagen & The Copenhagen Papers – Michael Frayn**

Michael Frayn's provocative play

*Copenhagen* explores a historical meeting between physicists Werner Heisenberg and Niels Bohr during World War II. In the context of wartime Copenhagen, the play explores the moral and ethical conundrums that scientists working on atomic research must overcome. With a fictional mystery involving misplaced manuscripts and academic intrigue, *The Copenhagen Papers* heightens the intrigue and demonstrates Frayn's skilful storytelling and profound connection to the city's intellectual legacy.

**Mount Copenhagen – Kaspar Colling Nielsen**

This novel tells the story of a 3,500-meter-tall mountain with a circumference of 55 km that appears out of nowhere on Denmark's flat terrain, drastically changing the topography and social structure of the nation. Nielsen investigates how the lives of common Danes are affected by this fantastical event, through a sequence of interconnected stories. With its witty social commentary and magical realism, the book provides a singular and engrossing look at modern Danish life.

**Helle Helle**

Celebrated Danish writer Helle Helle is renowned for her evocative and minimalist writing. Her books focus on the subtle complexities of ordinary life and are frequently set in small Danish towns and on the outskirts of Copenhagen. Helle's books are incredibly poignant and relatable because of her skill at capturing the subtleties of human emotions and interactions. *This Should Be Written in the Present Tense* and *Rødby-Puttgarden*, two of her best-known pieces, demonstrate her ability to craft compelling stories with a strong focus on the complexities of simple characters.

**Mirror, Shoulder, Signal – Dorthe Nors**

This smart, witty novel about a woman's driving lessons is a poignant, sharp-witted tale of one woman's journey in search of herself when there's no one to ask for directions. The story centres on Sonja, a middle-aged woman learning to drive while juggling the challenges of her personal life. The narrative provides an in-depth examination of personal development, self-discovery, and the difficulties of contemporary Copenhagen life. This novel captures the essence of modern urban life and is a compelling read thanks to Nors' astute observations and crisp, concise prose.

**Smilla's Sense of Snow – Peter Høeg**

A thrilling mystery, *Smilla's Sense of Snow*, takes readers on an exciting journey from the streets of Copenhagen to the icy landscapes of Greenland. The story follows Copenhagen-based Greenlander Smilla Jaspersen as she investigates the strange death of a young boy. A tense and engrossing reading experience is produced by Høeg's skilful storytelling and atmospheric descriptions of Copenhagen's wintry surroundings. The novel's examination of isolation and cultural identity gives this gripping thriller more nuance.

# FUN FACTS

### J-Dag

J-dag, short for *julebryg dag* (Christmas Brew Day), is a Danish tradition to mark the official launch of Tuborg's Christmas beer. It has become a highly anticipated event that essentially kicks off the Danish Christmas season. Taking place on the first Friday of November, it is celebrated in bars and on the streets. If you get lucky, you might spot the J-Dag lorry handing out free Christmas brews to try.

### Turning 25

Danes have interesting ways to celebrate milestones. If someone is single on their 25th birthday, their friends will drag them onto the street and likely tie them to a lamppost, covering them from head to toe in cinnamon. The same thing happens if they're unmarried at 30, only the cinnamon is replaced by black pepper.

### Graduation Traditions

In the last week of June, you will most likely find teenagers running around Copenhagen wearing the iconic student cap, *studenterhue*, which looks like a sailor's cap. It is awarded at completion of the final secondary school exam. All sorts of traditions are linked to the cap, such as different rules about what to write on and carve into it: e.g. if you see the sunrise while wearing it, you'll cut a triangle-shaped notch into its band. Open-back lorries filled with teenagers are driven around, playing loud music. This *studenterkørsel* lorry stops at every graduate's house, where

LEGO
LEDLITE
LEGO
Bag Tag
Étiquette
Pour Sac
Etiqueta
De Bolsa
KØBENHAVN

their family provides them with food and drinks.

### Liquorice everything

Danes are big fans of their liquorice, or *lakrids*, which often confuses foreigners as it is an acquired taste. However, Danes put it in everything, from ice cream and cocktails to cakes and savoury foods. Salted liquorice, often called *salmiak*, is a popular variety. Johan Bülow is a great brand, creating chocolate-covered liquorice in different flavours. If you visit the food market in the basement of Magasin du Nord, you're practically guaranteed to get a sample.

### Danish Inventions

Danes are innovative and research focused. They are pioneers in agriculture, medicine, and a range of other fields. LEGO is a popular Danish invention, which started with Ole Kirk Christiansen making wooden toys in 1932. The company is named after the Danish phrase *leg godt*, which means 'play well'. Skype and Google Maps are two more Danish inventions. It was also a Dane who helped discover insulin, as Hans Christian Hagedorn founded the Nordisk Insulin Laboratorium to establish its production.

### Safe & Happy

Denmark is continuously ranked one of the happiest countries in the world, and Copenhagen is often ranked as one of the most liveable cities. On top of that, it is also one of the safest. One thing you will immediately notice, which shows just how safe it is, are the babies left outside of restaurants, cafés, and shops to sleep in their prams. This is common practice in Denmark, as it is believed that it is healthy for babies to be outdoors and get as much fresh air as possible. And no one worries about their child being taken.

### Danish Islands

Denmark is made up of 444 islands, of which only 76 are inhabited. Many Danes use their summers to go on an island getaway to popular retreats such as Ærø, Rømø, Bornholm, and Læsø. In 2020, Bornholm and Samsø were voted the EU's most sustainable islands.

### Bicycles

Danes love to cycle. In 2020, Copenhageners owned five times more bikes than cars. It is estimated that combined, they cycle 1.44 million kilometres daily, and 49% of all trips to work or school in Copenhagen are taken by bike. All thanks to the cycling infrastructure in Copenhagen, which is designed to be both simple and safe.

↓ THE AUTHOR OF THIS GUIDE, MEREL, AT HER GRADUATION

# PHOTO SPOTS

**Nyhavn**

*Nyhavnsbroen, 1051 København K*

A touristy spot with a lot of picture-takers, the canal is still unmissable, lined with its colourful houses. The best place to take a picture of yourself is on Nyhavnsbroen, which allows you to pose with the buildings in the background. Visit late in the afternoon or in the evening to capture the golden-hour light, which reflects gorgeously off the boats and buildings.

**Operaparken**

*Ekvipagemestervej 18, 1438 København K, operaparken.dk*

The recently opened Opera Park, next to the Opera, offers stunning views of both its modern landscape architecture and the city's waterfront. The greenery gives a serene feel, and you can capture the gorgeous, winding structures surrounded by trees. Try framing the pathways behind the trees and plants to create a balanced and aesthetically pleasing picture. Alternatively, capture the grandeur of the Opera from the highest point of Operaparken, especially at night or during golden hour, when the harsh shadows are reduced, and a magical glow is added.

↓ DRONNING LOUISES BRO

↓ NYHAVN

↓ RUNDETÅRN

AiNE

**Rundetårn**

*Købmagergade 52A, 1150 København K, rundetaarn.dk*

The 17th-century Round Tower, which used to be an astronomical observatory, offers a unique spiral ramp. Capture the geometric beauty of the ramp from different angles as you ascend. Go at the end of the day, when the sun is not shining as brightly. This will make the light coming through the windows softer as you take your picture. Additionally, the top of the tower offers a panoramic view of the cityscape, showing a contrast between historic buildings and modern architecture.

**Nyboder**

*Sankt Pauls Gade 24, 1313 København K*

Nyboder is a historic district of yellow row houses built in the 17th century for the Danish Royal Navy. Their small doors and charming architecture make it a unique photo spot. Either capture the colourful doors and windows or create a repetitive pattern of the row houses to create a symmetrical composition.

**Palmehuset & Botanisk Have**

*Gothersgade 128, 1123 København K, snm.dk/en/botanical-garden*

The Botanical Gardens offer wonderful spots to capture some pictures. Use the water in the gardens to create reflective shots or focus on macro shots of the plants and flowers to highlight the vibrant colours and details. Within the Botanical Gardens, the Palm House, with its tropical plants and interesting iron detailing, creates a lush backdrop to your pictures. Also see page 49.

**Dronning Louises Bro**

*Søtorvet 2, 1371*
*København K*

A popular spot for locals to gather and enjoy views of the lakes. Try to capture the people relaxing and socialising on the bridge or use the calm water of the lakes to catch the reflections of the bridge and its surroundings. Alternatively, walk from this bridge to the next one on Gyldenløvesgade, where you can stand on the terrace next to Søpavilionen and get a more complete picture of the lakes as a backdrop.

**Cykelslangen**

*Cykelslangen, 1560*
*København V*

Cykelslangen is a modern, elevated cycling bridge connecting one part of the harbour to another. This 'Bicycle Snake' created by Dissing+Weitling architects gives an interesting shot, in which you can either capture the movement of the cyclists as they ride across, or to take a picture from the bridge itself to capture the magnificence of the Copenhagen Harbour.

**Tivoli Gardens**

*Vesterbrogade 3, 1630*
*København V, tivoli.dk*

Although you will have to pay an entrance fee, this is arguably one of the most versatile places to take pictures in Copenhagen. With its charming rides and beautiful gardens, this is a wonderful photo spot, especially at night. Use a wide angle on your camera to capture the grandeur of the park as a whole or try experimenting with a lower shutter speed to capture the flickering lights.

**Kartoffelrækkerne**

*Østerfarimagsgade,*
*2100 København Ø,*
*kartoffelraekkerne.dk*

Literally meaning the 'Potato Rows', Kartoffelrækkerne is a series of charming 19th-century worker's houses. The rows of maroon-brick homes with luscious green gardens are the perfect backdrop for a more casual picture. Shoot from the street level in a wide-angle to capture the continuity of the rows and the vibrant greenery.

# FOOD AND DRINKS

# BREAKFAST

### Sonny

This charming café is located near the city centre. It is known for its cosiness and delicious seasonal dishes. With a focus on quality ingredients, the menu features fresh salads, hearty sandwiches, and excellent coffee. The minimalist Scandinavian décor and outdoor terrace make it a perfect spot for a relaxing breakfast.

*Rådhusstræde 5, 1466 København K, sonnycph.dk*

### Kompa'9

If you want a delicious, light breakfast, this is the place to go. With their variations of eggs, yoghurt, and coffee and above all reasonable prices, this is a great place to grab a quick breakfast. The rustic, homely ambience and friendly service make it a favourite among locals and tourists alike.

*Kompagnistræde 9, 1208 København K, insta @kompa9cph*

### The Union Kitchen

Located in a side street of Nyhavn, this trendy eatery is known for its creative dishes and lively atmosphere. The menu offers a mix of international and Danish cuisine, with popular items like their signature meatballs and a variety of brunch options. The coffee is also known to be very Insta-worthy: cappuccinos are decorated with cacao creations ranging from Playboy Bunnies to inspirational quotes. The stylish interior and vibrant crowd make it an ideal spot for a social lunch. It can get very busy, so booking is a must.

*Shop Strandstræde 21, 1255 København K, theunionkitchen.dk*

## The Laundromat Café

The Laundromat has a real American diner feel, while maintaining the Danish *hygge* experience. Instead of plastic chairs, you'll find comfortable indoor and outdoor seats. With a menu featuring hearty breakfasts, pancakes, salads, and classic café fare, it's a great spot to relax and recharge. The quirky atmosphere, with its walls lined with books and colourful washing machines, adds to the charm.

*Århusgade 39, 2100 København Ø, thelaundromatcafe.com*

## Atelier September

This chic café and gallery space offers simple yet exquisite dishes. Known for its avocado toast and yoghurt with granola, this café emphasises fresh, high-quality ingredients. The bright, artistic interior creates a serene atmosphere, making it an excellent spot for a light, stylish breakfast. It is a good stop for your coffee to go as well.

*Århysgade 128, 2150 København Ø, cafeatelierseptember.com*

↓ 42 RAW, SEE PAGE 179

### Ø12

This café offers a modern take on traditional Danish *smørrebrød* (open-faced sandwiches), with a menu that highlights seasonal and organic ingredients. Located close to Sortedams Sø it provides a scenic backdrop for a relaxed lunch. The contemporary interior and focus on local produce make it a standout choice.

*Øster Farimagsgade 12b, 2100 København Ø, 12cph.dk*

### Wulff & Konstali

Go to Wulff & Konstali for delicious brunch plates and artisanal baked goods. The concept is especially interesting, as you can choose five or seven small plates for a set price. You mark your choices on the menu, which are then served to you on a lovely platter, ensuring a customised breakfast experience. With a focus on fresh, locally sourced ingredients, it's a perfect place for a leisurely breakfast.

*Sankt Hans Torv 30, 2200 København N, wogk.dk*

### Et Cetera

Come to Et Cetera if you're looking for something a little more adventurous for breakfast. The menu consists of Korean-inspired meals, with homemade kimchi and peanut noodles, or fluffy egg sandwiches. The building used to be a hair salon, which can still be felt through their eclectic decor, while remaining intimate and compact.

*Haraldsgade 3, 2200 København N, insta @etcetera.cph*

↓ RONDO

# CAFÉS & BAKERIES

Copenhagen is a real hotspot for bakeries where you can also get a coffee with your pastry. A classic Danish BMO or *bolle med ost* (roll with cheese) is a staple of Danish 'bread culture', a simple roll with cheese and butter. Danish bakery culture is rooted in tradition but constantly evolving, with most places selling classic Danish pastries or a contemporary twist on an old favourite.

**Hart Bageri**

Hart Bageri was founded by renowned baker Richard Hart, who previously worked at the famous Tartine Bakery in San Francisco. He opened this bakery in partnership with Noma's René Redzepi. Hart Bageri is celebrated for its artisanal bread, flaky croissants, and innovative pastries. Its minimalist design and warm atmosphere make it a perfect spot to enjoy freshly baked goods.

*Høkboderne 17, 1712 København K, hartbageri.com*

**Juno the Bakery**

This beloved neighbourhood bakery can be found in Østerbro. It is run by a Swedish owner, so it offers the perfect blend of Sweden and Denmark. It is famous for its cardamom buns, sourdough bread, buttery pastries, and seasonal saffron buns. The bakery's commitment to high-quality ingredients and traditional baking techniques – which you can see through the window – have earned it a loyal following. Be prepared for a queue, but the delicious treats are well worth the wait.

*Århusgade 48, 2100 København Ø, junothebakery.com*

## Rondo

Go to this small bakery in the heart of Copenhagen for high-quality baked goods and an inviting atmosphere. With a focus on organic ingredients and traditional baking methods, Rondo offers a variety of breads, pastries, and cakes that delight locals and visitors alike.

*Sjællandsgade 7, 2200 København N, rondo.dk*

## Ali Bageri

This hidden gem in the vibrant Nørrebro district is known for its delicious bread and pastries. Their slogan 'more than just bread' perfectly encapsulates the rich and diverse offerings Ali has. Its mostly Arabic food sets Ali Bageri apart from other bakeries in town. The bakery has a warm, welcoming vibe and is a local favourite for its quality and friendly service.

*Heimdalsgade 39, 2200 København N, alibageri.dk*

### Bageriet Benji

This café opened in May 2021, specialising in sourdough and pastries. It is the newest venture of Rasmus Kristensen, who was the head of bread and cakes at the world-famous Noma. The real stars of the show are their luxurious Spandauer pastries with marzipan and vanilla.

*Fælledvej 23, 2200 København N, insta @bageriet_benji*

### Flere Fugle

This bakery in the up-and-coming Nordvest area offers high-quality bread, pastries, and excellent coffee. Flere Fugle means 'several birds', reflecting its diverse offerings and friendly atmosphere. It's a great spot to enjoy a delicious pastry and a cup of coffee while soaking in the local vibe.

*Rentemestervej 57, 2400 København NV, flerefugle.dk*

## SMØRREBRØD

*Smørrebrød* is the classic Danish open-faced sandwich, and an edible experience of Danish design: where a carefully thought-out mix of textures, flavours, and colours is classically stacked on top of buttered rye bread.

### Schønnemann

This inviting cellar restaurant, which has been serving *smørrebrød* to Copenhageners for over a century, has won numerous awards. A framed cross-stitch picture on the wall tells of the days when this was a regular haunt for farmers and their dirty boots, with mud on the floor and herring on the table.

*Hauser Plads 16, 1127 København K, restaurantschonnemann.dk*

#### Selma

Selma offers a modern twist on the classic Danish dish and is currently the only *smørrebrød* restaurant in Copenhagen with a Bib Gourmand accolade. This is where you'll find creative and innovative sandwiches.

*Rømersgade 20, 1362 København K, selmacopenhagen.dk*

#### Restaurant Palægade

Palægade offers a sophisticated take on traditional Danish *smørrebrød*, set in an elegant yet welcoming environment. The restaurant is known for its dedication to preserving the authenticity of Danish cuisine with its herring-heavy menu.

*Palægade 8, 1261 København K, formelfamily.dk*

## LUNCH & DINNER

#### Corsa Pizza

There are four locations of Corsa in Copenhagen. The concept is simple yet delicious, and their stylish and light interiors make them great spots to spend a summer night in Copenhagen. Visit Corsa Pizza in Østerbro at Østerbrogade 56 to take out some slices and sit by the water to enjoy the sunset.

*corsapizza.dk*

↓ NORDIC HOTDOG AT REFFEN

### Hian

The best Vietnamese food in the city centre. With ample choice, between their various Phos and curries for only 79 DKK, there is bound to be something to your liking.

*Frederiksborggade 26, 1360 København K, hian.dk*

### District Tonkin

Although there are multiple locations, you should check out the one on Store Kongensgade, opposite the Marble Church. Dimly lit with neon signs, this Vietnamese restaurant is a hidden gem close to one of Copenhagen's most iconic sites.

*Store Kongensgade 71 København K, district-tonkin.dk*

### Fabro

With a handful of different antipasti and pastas, Fabro's concept is quite simple. The restaurant was created by a couple of friends to combine an informal style with homestyle cooking at a fair price. They don't take reservations, so expect to queue as it fills up quite quickly!

*Borgergade 134, 1300 København K, fabropasta.dk*

### Popl

The ingenious minds behind the popular Michelin restaurant Noma have created the delicious seasonally based burgers at POPL. This is the perfect neighbourhood spot to enjoy a simple but well-crafted burger. What started as a pop-up burger restaurant in the summer of 2020 is now permanently housed in the idyllic neighbourhood of Christianshavn.

*Strandgade 108, 1401 København K, poplburger.com*

### Petit Rouge

This restaurant's mission is for you to enjoy a delicious and filling meal without breaking the bank. Petit Rouge, located in a former shopping centre, is filled with modern art and antique pieces, a sentiment reflected in their menu, that lists French classics with modern twists.

*Kristen Bernikows Gade 9, 1105 København K, lepetitrouge.dk*

**Lola**

A little culinary trip around the world is guaranteed at Lola. This restaurant, located in an old mill in Christianshavn, embraces Latin American, Indian, and Southeast Asian influences, promising a flavourful exploration of global cuisines. But what really sets Lola apart is its ethos. A commitment to equality and well-being is reflected in their flat kitchen hierarchy, offering training and opportunities to those on the fringes of the labour market.

*Christianshavns Voldgade 54, 1424 København K, restaurantlola.dk*

**Magasasa**

Adored by both locals and tourists, and for good reason. It offers a spacious dining experience with an extensive menu. Favourites include the succulent roasted duck, flavourful pan-seared prawns, Dongpo pig shoulder, spicy tofu with minced beef, and the aromatic eggplant and minced pork cooked in a clay pot. Portions are generous and prices reasonable, leaving no room for complaints!

*Istedgade 4, 1650 København V, magasasa.dk*

**Mother**

One of the first restaurants to set up in the Meatpacking District (Kødbyen). They make their pizzas with purified seawater instead of traditional salt and water. These alternatives are healthier and tastier, resulting in simple, good soul food.

*Høkerboderne 9-15, 1712 København V, mother.dk*

↓ MINAS

↓ MEATPACKING DISTRICT

↓ MOTHER

### Paté Paté

This classic restaurant and wine bar in Copenhagen's Meatpacking District is housed in a former pâté factory. It is the area's oldest restaurant. The honest menu is written out on large blackboards. Prices are reasonable, and the wine menu is extensive. It is the perfect place for casual shared dining, with music playing on Fridays and Saturdays.

*Slagterboderne 1, 1716 København V, patepate.dk*

### Absalon

This colourful former church is much more than a restaurant. It is a social community house where *fællesspisning*, or shared dining, is at the centre. Check their website for their events calendar with theatre performances, bingo, and film nights. You can buy a ticket online in advance or try your luck at the door at 5pm. Dinner is 60 DKK Sundays to Wednesdays and 100 DKK on Thursdays, Fridays, and Saturdays.

*Sønder Boulevard 73, 1720 København V, absaloncph.dk*

### Palazzo Diner

You can find all-day breakfast in this modern take on a classic American diner. Swing by Sundays to Wednesdays to join their 'Pocket-Friendly Pasta Club', where you can feast on pasta dishes for just 89 DKK.

*Axeltorv 6, 1609 København V, palazzodiner.com*

### Bouillon

In the vibrant Frederiksberg neighbourhood, this Parisian-inspired eatery serves classic food at an affordable price. This includes French favourites such as onion soup, *tartare*, *steak frites*, and of course an amazing *mousse au chocolat* to end your French dining experience.

*Solbjergvej 3, 2000 Frederiksberg, restaurantbouillon.dk*

**Baest**

Bæst is 60-90% certified organic and they even produce their own burrata and ricotta. Choose from their range of à la carte pizzas or let yourself be surprised by the Bæst experience or the Bæst menu to experience tastings of pizza, charcuterie, and other small dishes.

*Guldbergsgade 29, 2200 København N, restaurantsafari.dk*

**Safari**

Simplicity meets joy in this blend of bar and restaurant, making it a great place to kickstart your evening out on the town. Dining here is informal, and their menu is filled with Central and Southern European bites.

*Baggesensgade 9, 2200 København N, restaurantsafari.dk*

**Hija de Sanchez Cantina**

The original Hija de Sanchez in Torvehallerne was proclaimed to be serving Europe's best street food in 2018. The head chef is a former dessert chef at Copenhagen's famous Noma restaurant, so expect the freshest sustainable ingredients, some sourced all the way from Mexico. Grab some tacos and enjoy the nearby Sandkaj Harbour bath or stay inside and enjoy the Scandinavian design with a hint of Mexico.

*Hamborg Plads 5, 2150 København N, lovesanches.com*

**Kini Kini**

Concrete and jungle elements are juxtaposed in this relaxed Indonesian restaurant in the newer neighbourhood of Nordhavn. It is a homage to both tropical Bali and the silos of Nordhavn.

*Göteborg Plads 9, 2150 København N, kinikini.dk*

# ICE CREAM

Good ice cream is as quintessentially Danish as Lego. You will find a staggering amount of ice-cream parlours in Copenhagen. In summer as well as winter, many of those will have people queuing outside.

### Ismageriet

Ismageriet in Amager offers freshly made Italian ice cream, produced in small batches throughout the day in their charming shop. Visitors can enjoy their creamy flavourful treats on a south-facing terrace that is furnished with classic Brunswick bowling benches. Despite the long queues, the variety of seasonal flavours and high-quality ingredients, including organic and fair-trade options, make the wait worthwhile.

*Flæsketorvet 45-55, 1711 København V, ismageriet.dk*

### Isoteket

The innovative, organic ice cream at Isoteket transports you from Østerbro to Italy. They are all about the perfect gelato with new flavour combinations and the best ingredients. Their authentic Italian gelato is made mostly with milk and some cream, resulting in a lighter texture.

*Randersgade 43, 2100 København Ø, isoteket.dk*

### Istid

The organic ice cream at Istid is made from fresh ingredients and liquid nitrogen. Founders Anniken and Nina have been creating ice-cold delights since 2015, offering a unique consistency that comes from their innovative freezing process. As the first in Scandinavia to use liquid nitrogen for ice cream, every occasion becomes a thrilling and delicious experience with their preparation that resembles a chemical experiment, and the thick clouds of white smoke.

*Jægersborggade 13, 2200 København N, istid.dk*

### Social Foodies

This small shop sells chocolate, ice cream, and chocolate-covered marshmallows, known as *fløddeboller*. Their focus is on 'doing good, better', which covers their socially aware approach to ice cream. Their products are made from high-quality raw materials, which, whenever possible, are grown and processed in Africa. This creates jobs that improve the living conditions of small farmers, locals, and their families.

*Sankt Hans Torv 24, 2200 København N, insta @social_foodies*

### Alice Ice Cream & Coffee

The mission at Alice is to make the very best ice cream, along-side out-of-this-world coffee and baked goods. From a tiny space on a side street off hectic Amagerbrogade, Alice serves ice cream made from prime ingredients, pushing the limits of what ice cream can be. Enjoy masterfully crafted baked goods and exceptional coffee from Swedish specialty roasters Koppi in a cosy, *hygge* atmosphere that makes Alice a year-round delight.

*Markmandsgade 1, 2300 København S, alicecph.dk*

## STREET FOOD

### Broens

Broens Gadekøkken combines street food kitchens with bars that serve international cuisine and beverages. Here you can enjoy world-class street food from renowned local restaurants and chefs who value quality, fresh ingredients, and excellent flavours. The Bridge Street Kitchen opened in May 2018 on the Greenlandic Trade Square at the end of Inderhavnsbroen. It started as a collaboration between the founders of Copenhagen Street Food – Papirøen and Reffen – and some of the owners of restaurant Noma. At Broens, you'll enjoy a range of food and drinks while overlooking the water, the Opera, and Nyhavn.

*Strandgade 95, 1401 København K, broens-streetfood.dk*

### Gasoline Grill

This must be the most talked-about burger joint in Copenhagen. The burger-to-go spot Gasoline Grill near Kongens Nytorv used to be a petrol station and now offers a simple but amazing burger. As Gasoline Grill even made it to Bloomberg's top 27 (!) best burgers in the world, there's often a queue for them. Don't let this scare you off, though, as the line moves quickly, and the burger is well worth the wait.

*Landgreven 10, 1300 København K, gasolinegrill.com*

### Reffen

Spring sees the re-opening of Reffen, Copenhagen's street food market on the former shipbuilding site of Refshaleøen. With its hangars and open waterfront space, it has become a destination for restaurants, urban farms, and art galleries; however, the street-food market, with international stalls in repurposed shipping containers, is its main attraction. Reffen is the largest in the Nordics. If the sun is out, you can sit on deckchairs overlooking the water while you tuck into local cuisine.

*Refshalevej 167, 1432 København K, reffen.dk*

### Torvehallerne

This indoor food market is one of Copenhagen's gems for specialty goods, fresh vegetables, and artisan food stalls. The two market halls are infused with scents from all corners of the world, coming from chain restaurants such as Grød to unique fish and cheese stands. Torvehallerne is right next to Nørreport Station, so it is a must if you're looking for a quick bite. If you're not in the mood for food, it is still a great place to stroll through to see the hustle and bustle of locals as well as vendors.

*Frederiksborggade 21, 1362 København K, torvehallernekbh.dk*

### John's Hotdog Deli

It's impossible to walk through the streets of Copenhagen and not come across a few hot dog stands. They are classic Danish. Any stand you come across offers good hot dogs for sure, but the best are sold at John's Deli, where the concept is slightly different to that of the average hotdog stand. John's hot dogs are served on durum bread made with butter, and you can choose from more than just your basic ketchup and mustard; they also have Mikkeller Beer Mustard, for instance.

*Bernstorffsgade 18, 1570 København V, insta @johns_hotdogdeli*

BAR
ROSÉ&SPRITZ

**Tivoli Food Hall**

The amusement park is one of the most visited attractions in Copenhagen, but the food hall next door is worth a visit in itself. Grab some coffee and baked goods at Brødflov, indulge in a modern take on the classic burger at Cocks and Cows, savour crispy pizzas at Gorm's, or enjoy grilled fast food at Bobbabella. It is budget-friendly, and you can grab food on the go or sit down to overlook Tivoli Gardens. It can get quite busy, so wait times may be longer. If you're looking for something more upscale, take the lift to the food hall roof. There, you'll find Sticks 'n Sushi, an excellent restaurant overlooking the gardens.

*Bernstorffsgade 3, 1577 København V, tivoli.dk*

**BaneGaarden**

A new green food and culture destination, created to provide a platform for sustainable development. Nine large old wooden barns, a greenhouse, and more than 1.5 hectares of wild nature make up BaneGaarden. A green oasis, ecological village, peaceful haven, and gastronomic centre. Away from the hustle and bustle, although still in the city centre, ideas grow wild, and projects sprout. The old barns, built by the Danish state railways in 1909, have been fully restored, and now house a food market, events, a cultural programme, restaurant, bakery and much more – all with the vision of contributing to the green transition through enthusiasm and inspiration rather than finger-pointing.

*Otto Busses Vej 45, 2450 København S, banegaarden.com*

## BRING THE PARENTS

**Boathouse**

At Christianshavn's waterfront, you'll find a serene and picturesque dining experience.

At Boathouse, California and Asian cuisines are beautifully combined with classic Danish dishes, with the menu reflecting and using both. We love the nautical feeling of this place.

*Strandgade 85, 1401 København K, boathouse.dk*

### The Market

A high-end Asian fusion restaurant close to Kongens Nytorv, with a variety of popular dishes from various Asian cuisines. The open kitchen creates a special atmosphere, and you can see how much passion the chefs put into the food. Their passion is also reflected in their *omakase*, a Japanese dining experience in which guests don't choose the dishes they have but leave these choices in the hands of the chef. Their range of cocktails offers options with sake, yuzu, and sakura. Next door, The Market also has an Italian restaurant.

*Kristen Bernikows Gade 11, 1105 København K, themarketcph.dk*

### The Silo

The Silo offers a dining experience like no other, featuring contemporary Danish cuisine mixed with French classics. You'll find it in the transformed Nordhavn grain silo, which now houses luxury apartments as well as this high-end restaurant. Situated on the 17th floor, The Silo provides stunning panoramic views of Copenhagen's skyline and harbour, making it the perfect spot for a memorable meal.

*Helsinkigade 29, 2150 København Ø, restaurantsilo.dk*

# GOING OUT

# BARS

### Camping Kødbyen

Go to Camping Kødbyen for a fun, slightly competitive, evening with friends or family. The bar serves tasty beers and cocktail pitchers, as well as delicious burgers and snacks from its partnership with the popular burger joint Cocks & Cows. Their main attraction is the creative sixteen-hole indoor mini golf course.

*Kødboderne 9, 1711 København K, camping.bar*

### Barkowski

Are you a fan of table football, pool, and darts? Go to Barkowski, a hip spot for young people, serving beer and wines at reasonable prices. You can also find board games and dice at this bar, and they screen sports events as well.

*Nørre Farimagsgade 57, 1364 København K, barkowskibar.dk*

### Bastard Café

On a rainy day, or if you are just in need of *hygge*, this is where to go. This games bar offers an assortment of over 3,800 board games and is staffed with game gurus who will help explain any game and get you started. The bar offers coffee, beer, and snacks, and it has a fifty per cent student discount.

*Rådhusstræde 13, 1466 København K, bastardcafe.dk*

### Det Elektriske Hjørne

This bar's name, which translates to 'Electric Corner', describes it perfectly. Det Elektriske Hjørne is a favourite in town, a popular corner bar located in central Copenhagen which offers indoor and outdoor seating. It is always filled to the brim! On Fridays and Saturdays, you can sit outside until 4am, or enjoy the music inside and dance the night away.

*Store Regnegade 12, 1110 København K, insta @elhjoernet*

**Studenterhuset**

This popular bar and café is affiliated with the University of Copenhagen and run by volunteers. It is a perfect meeting point for students and young professionals. During the day, the café is used for studying, while in the evenings, the bar hosts various activities such as concerts, a community kitchen, flea markets, and karaoke. In spring and summer, the cosy courtyard is opened, serving lots of different beers and wines at a student discount.

*Købmagergade 52, 1150 København K, studenterhuset.com*

**Farfars Bodega**

Classic *brune værtshuse* ('brown taverns'), are usually dimly lit pubs with an atmosphere created by their core of regulars and a focus on quality beers. A great example is Farfars Bodega in central Copenhagen, that allows you to experience authentic Danish pub culture, offering quizzes every Thursday, and all sorts of other fun events.

*Skindergade 20, 1159 København K, farfarbodega.dk*

**Sjus**

Located around the corner from Rundetårn, this bodega opens its doors seven days a week, serving cheap beers and other drinks. While the top floor offers a true bar experience, there's always a party on the intimate dance floor in the basement. Expect a range of fun activities in an authentic Danish atmosphere, with beers and liqueurs.

*Pilestræde 44, 1112 København K, sjusbar.dk*

↓ MIKKELLER BAR

↓ BRUS

↓ MIKKELLER BAR

↓ MIKKELLER BAR

### Nebbiolo Wine Bar

This restaurant/bar offers a wide array of self-imported Italian wines, with the opportunity to buy your favourite and take it home. Despite technically being in a tourist area, it is mostly frequented by locals, with few tourists to be seen. With rows of wine bottles lining the walls, the atmosphere at Nebbiolo is truly unique, and their delicious assortment of Italian antipasti just adds to the charm.

*Store Strandstræde 18, 1255 København K, nebbiolo-winebar.com*

### Balderdash

Founded by acclaimed mixologist Geoffrey Canilao, Balderdash offers a unique blend of classic and experimental cocktails. It is located in a small 1732 house with a secret door leading to the smaller assembly room. The venue also houses Geoffrey's own spirit lab and a gallery.

*Valkendorfsgade 11, 1151 København K, insta @balderdashcph*

### 1656 Cocktail Bar

This old-fashioned bar with classic chesterfield furniture and dimmed lighting offers customers seasonal cocktails as well as the good old classics. Located right next to the lively meatpacking district, this cocktail bar will have the skilled bartenders make you a drink with ingredients such as homemade apple syrup and melon puree, guaranteed to make your mouth water!

*Gasværksvej 33, 1656 København V, insta @1656cocktailbar*

### JOJO

This funky bar is known for their freshly produced and constantly changing cocktails, which they have on tap. It is arguably the best-priced bar in town, with cocktails for around 50 DKK. With its modern interior and colourful design and its location just a bike ride from the Meatpacking District, it is a very inviting place.

*Sundevedsgade 4, 1751 København V, jojovesterbro.dk*

**Mikkeller Bar**

As a world-renowned craft brewery, Mikkeller Bar is the place to go for the best Danish beer. Both the original bar in Vesterbro and their second location in Nørrebro offer Mikkeller tap beer, as well as other beers from the world's best breweries. They also serve some snacks, cheeses, and meats.

*Viktoriagade 8, 1655 København V, mikkeller.com*

**Mucki Bar**

An old-fashioned Danish bar, with a *hyggelig* atmosphere and delicious beer. It really gives the true Danish feel of a *brune værtshuse*, with its dark interior and strong alcohol scent. This classic bar even has its own song: check out *Mucki Bar* by Tobias Rahim.

*Thorsgade 5, 2200 København N, insta @mucki.bar*

**Léanowski**

Another classic student bar in Copenhagen, offering cheap drinks and all sorts of fun activities and games, which are free of charge. They also show screenings of football matches. Check out their website for their constantly changing calendar and catch a game or their next beer pong tournament.

*Fælledvej 21, 2200 København N, leanowskibar.dk*

**Vinhanen**

Vinhanen in Nørrebro has carved its own space in Copenhagen's vibrant wine scene. The concept is to keep prices low and the vibe easy-going, whilst still serving great wines. You can enjoy your wine, tapped from the large steel tanks, in-house, or buy some to go. On Mondays and Tuesdays, you can have *Le Petit Menu*, which includes one hot dish, one salad, and a glass of wine for 140 DKK.

*Baggesensgade 13, 2200 København N, vinhanen.dk*

### BRUS

The To Øl brewery offers an impressive selection of beers from up to 32 taps, and a little shop with non-alcoholic beverages. When the sun is out, the terrace will be packed with people from the neighbourhood. There is food too, think bao buns and a great double-smashed burger. Beer geeks can opt for a tasting or a brewery tour.

*Guldbergsgade 29, 2200 København N, tapperietbrus.dk*

## CLUBS

### Chateau Motel

A premier club and cocktail bar that boasts four floors, each dedicated to a different musical genre. From pulsating tech house to smooth R&B and vibrant Afrobeat, there's something to ignite everyone's party spirit. Situated in the heart of Copenhagen, this nightclub is impossible to miss. On entering the courtyard, you'll be greeted by impressive light installations and art. This vibe continues inside with striking decorations, and walls as well as ceilings covered in lights and mirrors.

*Knabrostræde 3, 1210 København K, chateaumotel.dk*

### Arch

A glamorous interior design, great music, and a lively atmosphere. Arch boasts a popular line-up, having hosted world-renowned DJs, such as Diplo and DJ Snake. Arch is known for its slightly exclusive allure, so it's definitely a night to dress up and look your best.

*Nørregade 41, 1165 København K, archcph.com*

### Søpavillonen

Known for both its vibrant community and stunning location overlooking the lakes, going to Søpavillonen, or as the Danes call it 'Sø', is always a good idea. Housed in the same building, family restaurant Babylon serves gourmet seafood and delicious desserts. As to be expected, the queues for this club can get very long. Tip: book for dinner or drinks at the restaurant and then wait until the nightclub opens.

*Gyldenløvesgade 24, 1369 København K, soepavillonen.dk*

**Culture Box**

An electronic music lover's dream, open to anyone over 18, without a dress code. The entrance fee includes a complimentary first drink. Since its opening in 2005, Culture Box has showcased both international and local artists from the underground music scene. As an added bonus, you can rave until 8am on weekends!

*Kronprinsessegade 54, 1306 København K, culture-box.com*

**Sigurd**

Dance until the sun comes up in this club in outer Nørrebro! The venue attracts a youthful student crowd creating an exciting and energetic atmosphere – and the queue usually is shorter than at other clubs. All events are 21+, so keep this in mind if you're planning to go. They also have an outdoor venue called Sigurd Haven, and a wine bar called Sigurd Vinbaren, which are accessible on weekdays for those under 21.

*Sigurdsgade 39, 2200 København N, sigurdcph.com*

**Rust**

A bar during the week and a club on weekends, this is the perfect combination of conviviality and fun. This intimate live music venue in Nørrebro hosts live concerts every Friday and Saturday, with music ranging from DJ acts to hip hop and R&B. After 11pm the bar turns into a nightclub, and the party really gets started.

*Guldbergsgade 8, 2200 København N, rust.dk*

LEACOCK'S
SAINT JOHN
MADEIRA

# SHOPPING

# HOW TO DRESS LIKE A LOCAL

Copenhagen is not only a hub for innovation and design, but also a fashion capital with a chic, sustainable, and laid-back style. This blend of comfort, practicality, and a touch of quirkiness can be traced back to the idea of *hygge*.

'Normcore' style, characterised by unpretentious clothes, is frequently seen in Copenhagen. This includes a pair of baggy jeans and a nice wool jumper to wear throughout the year. Casual is key, but so is contrast: think trainers with a suit or baggy jeans with high heels. This has been coined by Allison Bornstein as the 'wrong' shoe theory. Accessories will include statement necklaces or quirky earrings or a colourful bag.

Layers are the key to surviving Copenhagen's ever-changing weather and a good rule of thumb is that carrying extra layers with you in summer, or bringing thermals in winter is never a bad idea. In winter, you will come across a variety of scarves ranging from oversized to small, but always practical. Wool socks and a chunky jumper are a given. During the colder months, you might see adults wearing a one-piece that looks like the ones small children would wear to play outside, and this is the perfect mix of staying stylish while staying warm. Additionally, Danes like to invest in practical pieces such as raincoats or wellies, as to them good quality pieces are worth their price to stay stylish while being practical. The colour palette seen in Copenhagen is usually quite minimalist, with some neutral tones and colours, often black, navy, charcoal, and beige.

# FLEA MARKETS

Copenhagen truly is a vintage lover's treasure trove. In many areas such as Vesterbro and Nørrebro, you'll find vintage and second-hand shops dotted around. And there is also a vibrant flea market culture, with the markets as a popular weekend activity for young and old.

**Københavns Loppetorv**

*Israels Plads, 1361 København K, kbhloppetorv.dk*

'Make Green Sense' is the motto of Copenhagen's Loppetorv, which is open every Saturday from April through October 11am to 4pm. Everything from socks to armchairs can be found. On their themed Saturdays, they focus on a particular category, and you can find exactly what you're looking for.

**Vera's Marked Under Buen**

*Bispeengen 12, 2000, Frederiksberg, verasvintage.dk*

One of the most popular flea markets in Copenhagen by far, and the focus is especially on high-quality second-hand clothes. Individual sellers often sell high-end brands like Ganni, Mads Nøgaard, Ralph Lauren, essentially anything popular among Copenhagen girls. The market runs Sundays 9am-3pm, regardless of the weather, as the stands are covered by the bridge that runs over the flea market. As a bonus, there is always music playing to enhance your shopping experience.

**Loppetorv at Frederiksberg**

*Frederiksberg Bredegade, 2000 Frederiksberg, insta @ frederiksbergloppemarked*

Saturdays from April to October, you'll find this bustling flea market held between 9am and 3pm right by Frederiksberg City Hall. As it is an upscale neighbourhood, items sold at Frederiksberg Loppetorv are typically of high quality, making it a good place for good finds at affordable prices.

**Det Grønne Loppemarked**

*Nørrebroruten, 2200 København N, detgroenneloppemarked.dk*

This flea market has a collection of individual resellers as well as curated stands with spices, books, and plants. The 'Green Flea Market' aims to set itself apart by embracing the idea of a 'market day' where you can buy organic vegetables, sourdough bread, plant-based breakfast and lunch, and participate in sustainability workshops. There is also plenty of prepared food to find.

**Gentofte Loppemarked**

*Bregnegårdsvej 2, 2920 Charlottenlund, gentofteloppemarked.dk*

This flea market is open every Sunday from 8am to 2pm, regardless of the weather. You can find it right next to the Charlottenlund train station. At this flea market, you can also score gems such as furniture, homeware, and records, in addition to clothes.

# VINTAGE & SECOND-HAND

**Magnolia's Luksus 2ndhand**

*Købmagergade 5, 1150 København K, magnolias2ndhand.dk*

In the basement underneath a hat shop on Købmagergade, you'll find Magnolia's, which is at the top of of every vintage lover's list in Copenhagen. This shop carries consignment and second-hand clothes that can range from brands like Ganni to Louis Vuitton. It is especially known for its designer handbags and shoes.

**Time's Up Vintage**

*Krystalgade 4, 1172 København K, timesupshop.com*

Everything you see is sourced by founder and owner Jesper Richardy during his many travels, with a focus on quality and long-lasting pieces. In this shop you'll find rare vintage and collectible designer pieces, giving it a more upscale feel than many others.

**O-S-V Secondhand**

*Peder Hvitfeldts Stræde 4, 1173 København K, osvsecondhand.com*

The owners of O-S-V wanted to create an environment that focuses on equality and being welcoming. This is why the shop has an equal focus on women's clothes and menswear, and is the first luxury vintage shop in Copenhagen to do so. There's an in-shop café for customers to grab a coffee and stay as long as they like. O-S-V is short for *og så videre*, 'and so on', capturing the brand's commitment to circularity.

**Palette 26**

*Hyskenstræde 9, 1207 København K, palette26.com*

This shop has a smaller, meticulously curated collection of second-hand pieces, and truly has something fun for everyone. Its name refers to their broad 'palette' of handmade ceramics and vases, their vintage products, and a colourful painter's palette filled with nuances. Their goal is to create more interest in small businesses, craftsmanship, and local production, paving the way for a more personal connection between producer and customer.

**Strand 32**

*Strandgade 32, 1402 København K*

This shop is easily missed as it is quite unassuming from the outside. The inside, however, is a completely different story. Once you descend the stairs, you'll immediately see their large collection of second-hand shoes. The racks may seem to tower over you, but each corner is packed with one-of-a-kind hidden gems waiting to be discovered.

**Carmen Copenhagen**

*Larsbjørnssstræde 5, 1454 København K, insta @carmen.cph*

Larsbjørnssstræde, an area full of quirky shops, houses Carmen Copenhagen, one of the city's oldest vintage shops. It stocks clothes for women as well as men, with a focus on the 1970s and 1980s. Other finds include bags, hats, coats and jewellery.

WELC
TO Fab
LAS V
NEVA

**Quirky Lane**

*Studiestræde 15, 1455 København K, insta @quirkylanecph*

On a street with many vintage shops, Quirky Lane stands out due to its commitment to colour. Not only is the interior of the shop lined with pink and warm lighting, but the clothes also stand out for their bright colours and eclectic designs. With bold patterns and colours, this is the place to find a statement piece or a quirky addition to your wardrobe.

**Wasteland**

*Studiestræde 19, 1455 København K, wasteland.dk*

Wasteland has a collection of everything you could possibly imagine getting your hands on, from cocktail dresses with funky prints and sparkles, to retro jewellery, to Ralph Lauren vintage jumpers and Levi's jeans. Wasteland sets itself apart from other vintage and second-hand shops in Copenhagen by bulk ordering second-hand clothes from the US and Canada, which is evident from their large collection of sports jerseys and classic vintage varsity jackets.

**Veras**

*Studiestræde 27, 1455 København K, verasvintage.dk*

Not just a shop you just walk into to buy something. Veras has an exchange concept, meaning they place a value on any clothes you bring in, and with that credit you can buy new items, revolutionising the idea of circular clothing. You can buy clothes without exchanging, though.

**Kilo Vintage Sale**

*Vesterbrogade 52, 1620 København V, kilovintagesale.com*

Buy vintage clothes the way you would buy sweets at a sweets shop, by paying at a price per kilo. You can find out the weight of your items before you check out, so you don't have to worry about not knowing what you are paying, and you don't have to buy a whole kilo either.

**Lidkøb**

*Strynøgade 7, 2100 København Ø, lidkob.dk*

Lidkøb is a hybrid of a flea market and a second-hand shop. People who want to give their clothes a second life can have their items displayed, but Lidkøb will sell them for a take of the earnings. So, you'll see a range of clothes from individual sellers, all managed by one shop. Lidkøb has great variety and fair prices.

**Keiko**

*Birkegade 9A, 2200 København N, insta @keikocph, TikTok @keikovintage*

Located in Nørrebro on a street with a lot of vintage shops, Keiko offers a vibrant shopping experience, standing out with their lively and exciting window displays. This shop often has sales on top of the already affordable prices, so make sure to keep an eye on their socials for the latest developments. Keiko is filled with cowboy vintage, unique pieces, belts, and an eclectic mix of fashion gems from various decades. You'll find everything from retro denim jackets and bohemian dresses to stylish hats and statement jewellery.

**Second Wardrobe**

*Egegade 2, 2200 København N, insta @second_wardrobe_by_martine*

For upscale pre-loved women's clothes, accessories, and shoes, Second Wardrobe is another go-to. The boutique features classic pieces from luxury labels alongside the newest fashions. Second Wardrobe offers an extensive selection of excellent items at reasonable prices, whether you're looking for unique vintage pieces or sold-out items from brands such as Burberry, Ganni, and Arket. Check out their Instagram to stay aware of their newest collections and exclusive deals, and find out to see what's in stock and what was already sold, along with the original prices.

**Røde Kors Megastore**

*Fælledvej 4, 2200 København N, insta @rodekorsmegastore*

This is your classic Red Cross charity shop that carries anything you can think of, from furniture and books to kitchenware to clothes. Shopping at their megastore does not only allow you to find unique and stylish pieces, but also contributes to a charitable cause. The shop's atmosphere reflects the community-focused mission of the Red Cross.

**Prag**

*Nørrebrogade 45, 2200 København N, pragcopenhagen.dk*

This second-hand shop is known for being amazingly organised, turning a stressful second-hand shopping experience into a satisfying one. Clothes are not only sorted by type but there is a subdivision: your silk trousers, chinos, and jeans are all separated so you don't have to go through everything to find what you're looking for. Prag also has great accessories, such as a good collection of hair clips and jewellery.

**Crush Vintage**

*Nørrebrogade 5, 2200 København N, insta @crush.copenhagen*

Cowboys and cowgirls, this one is for you: Crush Vintage! One of the most colourful vintage shops in town and a great spot for lots of denim, cowboy boots, festival outfits, jewellery, and much more. Spin the wheel for discounts.

**Kabomani**

*Amagerbrogade 48 st. 3, 2300 København S, tapirus.dk*

Formerly known as Tapirus, Kabomani sells and buys pre-loved pieces for both men and women. This truly is a hidden gem on Amager, a little bit off the beaten track. Along with fun vintage pieces and lesser-known gems, you can find trendy Scandinavian clothes, accessories, shoes, and jewellery.

↓ RED KORS

# STREETWEAR

**Storm**

*Store Regnegade 1, 1110 København K, stormfashion.dk*

Storm is a cultural institution within Copenhagen's fashion scene, much more than just a shop. The city centre shop looks more like a showroom, with a unique blend of streetwear, high fashion, and lifestyle items. The shop offers a variety of books, magazines, and artwork in addition to labels like Off-White, Rick Owens, and Raf Simons. For anyone interested in streetwear, Storm is a must-visit because of its cutting-edge selection and inventive approach to retail.

**Boii Studios**

*Kronprinsensgade 5, 1114 København K, boiistudios.com*

Boii has the best blend of high-quality basics and statement pieces like skirts, dresses, and blouses. The shop focuses on sustainability and ethical production, reusing fabrics, and using the same fabrics for multiple items. Leftover fabrics are usually used to make nifty toiletry bags. Boii often has great sales and offers a pleasant shopping experience if you want to get some truly Danish-styled pieces.

**Ganni Postmodern**

*Overgaden Oven Vandet 40, 1415 København K, ganni.com*

Ganni is renowned for its playful and colourful aesthetic, which combines classic silhouettes with colourful patterns. Customers can find classic Ganni items capturing the brand's quirky and modern style in the Archive Store in

Christianshavn. It's a terrific place to find eye-catching pieces that give any outfit a distinctive flair.

**Mads Nørgaard**

*Amagertorv 13-15, 1160 København K, madsnorgaard.com*

Danish fashion icon Mads Nørgaard is renowned for his timeless yet contemporary designs that perfectly capture the essence of Scandinavian minimalism. A large selection of clothes for men and women is available at the brand's flagship store on Amagertorv, including the versatile outerwear and striped tops that are the brand's signatures.

**Naked Copenhagen**

*Store Regnegade 2, 1110 København K, nakedcph.com*

This shop curates cool trainers and streetwear that are especially catered to empowering women. Naked has access to all major brands' most exclusive tiers and often stocks limited releases from brands like Nike, New Balance, adidas, and Salomon.

**Won Hundred**

*Gammel Kongevej 102, 1850 Frederiksberg, wonhundred.com*

A Danish fashion label with origins in the Scandinavian minimalist design tradition and denim design. Won Hundred offers practical apparel for men and women that emphasises wearable items for daily life, such as an eco-friendly clothing line. Known for its clean lines and understated elegance, Won Hundred's pieces are both stylish and functional, and the brand is committed to high-quality materials and ethical production.

# DEPARTMENT STORES

**Magasin du Nord**

*Kongens Nytorv 13, 1095 København K, magasin.dk*

With its elegant architecture and extensive range of products, Magasin du Nord offers a luxurious shopping experience. Browse through floors of high-end fashion, beauty products, gourmet food, and home deco. Each Christmas, Magasin du Nord's façade features wonderful lights and decorations, so make sure to check it out if you are visiting in winter!

**Illum**

*Østergade 52, 1100 København K, illum.dk*

Illum, on Copenhagen's main shopping street Strøget, is another top destination for shoppers. This stylish department store is known for luxurious brands and modern Scandinavian design. There are a number of restaurants and cafés on the top floor, where you can enjoy a meal or drink with unrivalled views of Strøget and Christiansborg Palace.

**Fisketorvet – Copenhagen Mall**

*Kalvebod Brygge 59, 1560 København V, fisketorvet.dk*

Fisketorvet, which hosts more than 120 shops and offers everything you could think of in true 'mall' style, is one of the largest and most popular shopping destinations in Copenhagen, located right by the waterfront.

**Waterfront Shopping**

*Philip Heymans Alle 17, 2900 Hellerup, waterfront-shopping.dk*

A little bit out of central Copenhagen, in the upscale neighbourhood of Hellerup, Waterfront Shopping offers a shopping experience. This shopping centre boasts sleek, contemporary design, with some restaurants overlooking the harbour. After shopping here, take a walk around Tuborg Harbour, which has a history of beer brewing visualised with two large beer bottles on either end of the harbour.

↓ MAGASIN DU NORD

# BOOKSHOPS

**New Mags**

*Ny Østergade 28, 1101 København K, new-mags.com*

This is a haven for those who appreciate the art of stylish literature. New Mags takes inspiration from traditional libraries, creating a peaceful and sophisticated space celebrating books as works of art on their own right. The interior's design with oak and other natural materials is a thoughtful touch to enhance your browsing experience.

**Arnold Busck**

*Købmagergade 49, 1150 København K, jppol.dk*

With multiple locations throughout Copenhagen, Arnold Busck is one of the biggest and most established book chains in Denmark. The flagship store on Købmagergade is a large, expansive area brimming with gifts, stationery, and books. Arnold Busck is well-known for its extensive collection and knowledgeable staff. It offers books for all interests, including children's books, academic texts, contemporary fiction, and classic literature.

**Le Petit Voyeur**

*Sølvgade 5, 1307 København K, lepetitvoyeur.com*

This is one of those shops that you can't pass by without turning your head for an extra glance. With its cool and inviting exterior, this bookshop is a magnet for lovers of independent visual arts publications from around the world. Specialising in limited and signed editions, Le

Petit Voyeur offers a unique experience where you can easily lose track of time exploring the eclectic selection. Make sure to check their opening hours, as they can be limited.

**Cinnober**

*Landemærket 9,*
*1119 København K,*
*cinnoberbookshop.dk*

Independent bookshop and gallery Cinnober is close to historic Copenhagen. For those with an intense interest in visual culture, this upscale bookshop is a must-visit as it specialises in books on art, craft, and design. The shop stocks both local and international publications, and its impressive selection of titles caters to professionals, students, and enthusiasts alike.

↓ THIEMERS MAGASIN

**Thiemers Magasin**

*Tullinsgade 24, 1618 København V, thiemersmagasin.dk*

The shop's intimate setting, complete with a small café, creates a welcoming environment for book lovers to gather and discuss their favourite reads. Thiemers Magasin's mission is to curate a collection of books for their literary quality, societal relevance, and daringness.

**Politikens Boghal**

*Rådhuspladsen 37, 1785 København V, jppol.dk*

Also known as Boghallen, located in the heart of Copenhagen near Rådhuspladsen, Politikens Boghal is a well-loved institution for book enthusiasts. It's part of the iconic Politikens Hus, home to one of Denmark's leading newspapers. Boghallen offers an extensive selection of Danish and international books, magazines, and newspapers. The shop's inviting atmosphere makes it a perfect spot to browse for hours.

**Super Time Books**

*Blågårdsgade 31C, 2200 København N, supertimebooks.com*

An independent bookshop which prides itself on independent publications and project-based collaborations, allowing writers to send in manuscripts, honouring their slogan, 'you write, we publish'. They also organise events such as reading soirées and drawing workshops. Even if you are not a writer yourself, they have a very welcoming, friendly vibe with a small but interesting selection of books targeted mainly to creatives.

**Ark Books**

*Møllegade 10, 2200 København N, arkbooks.dk*

Ark Books is a non-profit volunteer-run international bookshop. This bookshop, with a diverse range of English-language literature, focuses on fiction but also includes selections of poetry and critical theory, with an emphasis on independent and small-press publications.

**Storrs Antikvariat**

*Frederikssundsvej 61, 2400 København NV, storrsantikvariat.dk*

Nestled between a pizza place and a butcher's shop, this is the place for bookworms to find their second-hand books. Among the 5,000 books, there is a small selection of English titles, and visiting it is an experience.

**Books & Company**

*Sofievej 1, 2900 Hellerup, booksandcompany.com*

This English-language bookshop in Hellerup is conveniently located just north of the city centre and has grown to be a favourite among both locals and visitors. A carefully chosen assortment of English-language books, including children's books, fiction, and non-fiction, is available at this quaint independent bookshop. It's the ideal spot to unwind with a good book and a cup of coffee because of the welcoming ambiance and small café. Books & Company also regularly hosts children's storytelling sessions, book clubs, and author talks.

# ART SUPPLIES

**Muji**

*Østergade 52, 1100 København K, muji.com*

Japanese retailer Muji is well-known for its premium goods and minimalist style, and it is quite prevalent in Copenhagen. This versatile shop is located on the top floor of the Illum department store and despite not being a conventional art supply shop, Muji has a variety of goods that are ideal for crafters and artists. Premium sketchbooks, pens, markers, and other stationery items are available. Muji's focus on functionality and simplicity makes it a favourite with people who value well-made, useful tools for their artistic endeavours.

**Panduro Hobby**

*Nørre Farimagsgade 74, 1364 København K, panduro.com*

Panduro is your one-stop shop for all things hobby and creativity. Here you can buy yarn, DIY kits, paint, and whatever else you can think of to get the creativity flowing.

**Creative Space**

*Kastelsvej 1, 2100 København Ø, creative-space.dk*

Unlike traditional art supply shops, Creative Space provides a unique, hands-on experience to create your own ceramic masterpieces. The idea is straightforward but captivating: pick out a piece of pottery, paint it with any of the available colours and tools, and let it dry and be fired. Make sure to book ahead and leave enough time for your artwork to dry and be picked up!

**Uldstedet**

*Vendersgade 3, 1363 København K, uldstedet.dk*

With a wide variety of basic as well as high-end yarns, this shop is bustling all the time. It is a must-visit for any knitting or crochet fanatics. There is an array of samples available, so you can test out the yarns before buying.

**Flying Tiger**

*flyingtiger.com*

One-stop shopping for home deco, notebooks, pens, pencils, and much more. You might know the shop from your hometown, but as it is a Copenhagen brand, you should pop in anyway. There are various shops all around town.

# DANISH DESIGN & MORE

**Søstrene Grene**

*Amager Torv 24, 1160 København K, sostrenegrene.com*

There might be a Søstrene Grene where you live, but visiting the shop on Strøget is a must. This Danish chain has a wealth of elegant products with Nordic origins for a revamp of your home, whether small or large. The focus is on the natural joy and aesthetics of the little things in life, and many items have been designed by the sisters Anna and Clara themselves. This shop has a slide taking you from the first floor to the ground floor, so it's going to be a fun visit.

**Notre Dame**

*Nørregade 7, 1165 København K, notredame.dk*

In central Copenhagen, you'll find a quaint lifestyle and home deco shop called Notre Dame. It sells a carefully chosen range of fashionable yet reasonably priced goods, such as lighting, textiles, small furniture, and tableware. Notre Dame is renowned for superior products that infuse any home with a hint of elegance and a Scandinavian aesthetic.

**Posterland**

*Gothersgade 45, 1123 København K, posterland.dk*

This two-story shop is the largest poster, art print, and postcard retailer in Northern Europe. The shop has a great selection of retro and modern posters of Copenhagen, as well as photographs of the city. A great souvenir to bring back home and pimp up your space!

**HAY House**

*Østergade 61, 1100 København K, hay.dk*

The flagship store of the well-known Danish design brand HAY is housed in a stunning historic building in the heart of Copenhagen. A large selection of modern lighting, accessories, and furniture is available in the shop. You can still add a touch of Danish design to your home without going over budget with many of the smaller pieces, such as trays, cushions, and storage options.

**Illums Bolighus**

*Amagertorv 10, 1160 København K, illumsbolighus.com*

The flagship store of Illums Bolighus is located at Amagertorv square, right around the corner from the Illum department store. This unique shop mixes famous classic Danish design with modern twists. Additionally, Illums Bolighus is a provider to the Royal Danish Court, making this THE place to go buy some real Danish design pieces, or to just enjoy the various interior decorations on sale.

**Retro Villa**

*Vennemindevej 28, 2100 København Ø, retrovilla.dk*

Specialised in one-of-a-kind home deco items and vintage wallpaper. The shop is a great place to find unique pieces to add character to your home, as it offers an eclectic mix of retro and contemporary designs. Retro Villa has a variety of reasonably priced options, especially in their selection of wallpapers and smaller deco items, even though some vintage items can be pricey.

# RECORD SHOPS

**Accord**

*Vesterbrogade 63, 1620 København V, accord.dk*

The oldest record shop in Copenhagen has a long and illustrious past that goes back to the 1940s. More than 50,000 vinyl records are available at the Vesterbro location, which also has a special pricing structure with bargain bins where you can find one record for 30 DKK and four for 100 DKK. Accord's basement with its vast assortment of Danish records and soundtracks is a real gold mine. The records are only opened for listening after being sealed in-house, meaning their condition is generally very good.

**Sound Station**

*Gammel Kongevej 94, 1850 Frederiksberg, soundstation.dk*

One of Scandinavia's best-stocked record shops, and a real establishment for vinyl enthusiasts in Copenhagen. It has a great assortment of pop, rock, indie, jazz, and new releases. The breadth of stock and the condition of the neatly arranged records are excellent, which accounts for the relatively high prices. Additionally, they highlight recently released pop and dance music from independent labels.

**Ooh Aah Records**

*Ryesgade 77, 2100 København Ø, oohaahrecords.com*

This shop in Nørrebro focuses on punk rock but also offers a variety of genres including progressive rock, experimental, electronic, disco, and soul. Tim's personal touch includes a rack of Pendleton wool shirts from his U.S. trips. Ooh Aah Records is a cosy spot with around four thousand records, where Tim eagerly plays vinyl for his customers. He tries to support local artists and new musicians, although his core business remains dealing in used records.

**Second Beat**

*Jagtvej 129, 2200 København N, secondbeat.dk*

Owned by Nils Rolfgaard, a local enthusiast, Second Beat is a vibrant record shop with an ever-changing inventory. Nils makes sure there's always something new to discover, offering jazz, soul, reggae, and Danish music in addition to his specialty, rock and pop. Nils adds a personal touch by playing records on the shop's hi-fi system, even though there isn't a listening booth. The shop's eclectic charm is further enhanced by a carefully chosen assortment of books and collectibles.

# SHOPS WE LOVE

**Sui Ava**

*Gammel Mønt 23, 1117 København K, suiava.dk*

The place to go for fun and fashionable hair accessories. The shop, which was founded by a mother of two energetic daughters, Sui and Ava, embodies a passion for life and a willingness to take risks. Motivated by joyful curiosity, the creator brings fun to each piece. The shop has developed a cult following thanks to its bright and fun headbands, hair clips, and other accessories that liven up any ensemble.

**Studio Arhøj**

*Skindergade 7, 1159 København K, arhoj.com*

Danish design company Studio Arhøj creates one-of-a-kind ceramic pieces by fusing traditional Scandinavian and Japanese design elements. Situated in the heart of Copenhagen, this shop offers an abundance of exquisitely designed goods, ranging from vases and cups to unique figurines and home deco. Since each item is handmade, no two will be the same.

**Aiayu**

*Store Strandstræde 12a, 1255 København K, aiayu.com*

A Copenhagen-based brand known for its luxurious and sustainable clothes, home textiles, and accessories. The brand emphasises sustainability, using natural fibres and ethical production methods, and they are of the firm belief that plastic should not be on our bodies. From cosy knitwear and soft bedding to timeless wardrobe staples, Aiayu's products are designed to be cherished and enjoyed for years. Their focus on quality and sustainability makes Aiayu a standout in Copenhagen's retail scene.

**Norr**

*Pilestræde 36, 1112 København K, norrofficial.dk*

At Norr you can find all the hip Danish brands in one spot. This is where you go to infuse your wardrobe with some Scandinavian elegance, and it's overall a fun shop to visit, with its koi pond and chic and modern interior. You can also find plenty of accessories and trinkets for your home.

**Planet Nusa**

*Gammel Kongevej 136, 1850 Frederiksberg, planetnusa.com*

Planet Nusa is a female-owned sustainable sportswear company that specialises in producing premium environmentally responsible training apparel. Their Frederiksberg shop sells a variety of fashionable and useful items crafted from recycled materials. Planet Nusa offers a wide selection of comfortable loungewear, sports bras, and leggings to meet your needs. The brand is well-liked by customers for its dedication to sustainability and ethical production methods. The contemporary and minimalistic designs of Planet Nusa are ideal for daily wear as well as exercise.

GREEN COPENHAGEN

# PARKS

### Kongens Have

Kongens Have, which translates to 'King's Garden', is also known as the Rosenborg Castle Gardens and is one of Copenhagen's oldest and best-known parks. Situated in the heart of the city, it boasts immaculately tended lawns, paths bordered by trees, and vivid flower beds. A bit of historical charm is added by the moat of Rosenborg Castle. It's the ideal location for strolls, picnics, and taking in the changing floral displays.

*Øster Voldgade 4A, 1307 København K*

### Fælledparken

Copenhagen's largest park has a lot to offer in terms of amenities and activities. It has areas for grilling, sports fields, a skate park, and playgrounds, and you'll often find little coffee carts to get your caffeine fix. Locals gather in this bustling area for sporting events, picnics, and other occasions throughout the year, such as the annual Copenhagen Carnival. From here, you can easily walk to the Copenhagen Lakes, which are around the corner, and provide a nice space for a stroll. However, you can't swim in the lakes.

*Fælledparken, 2100 København Ø*

### Amager Fælled

A little outside the city centre you'll find Amager Fælled, a large natural area with a variety of wetlands, wooded areas, and wild meadows. Amager Fælled is perfect for birdwatching, cycling, and hiking. The park is the ideal retreat for nature lovers because of its unspoiled natural beauty, which is a lovely contrast to the city.

*Artillerivej 73B, 2300 København S*

↓ BOTANISK HAVE, SEE PAGE 49

# SWIMMING

### Ofelia Plads

Ofelia Plads, which is an official swimming spot, offers a wonderful view of the Opera House. You can lounge on the wooden boards, and it is conveniently located in the city centre, close to Nyhavn.

*Kvæsthusbroen, 1250 København K*

### Refshaleøen

There are multiple swimming spots on Refshaleøen. With the huge street food market in the background, you can enjoy a dip south of the street food area with ladders to get in and out (Søndre Refshalebassin). Alternatively, you can visit La Banchina (Refshalevej 141), a restaurant with its own bathing pier, around the corner from Reffen Food Market.

*Refshalevej 145A, 1432 København K*

### Svanemøllen Beach

A man-made beach close to the city centre of Copenhagen, so you can lounge in the sand or jump off the pier into deeper waters. After having a dip, you can take in the views of the yachts at the Svanemøllen marina, which is a great spot to have an ice cream after your swim.

*Strandpromenaden 30, 2100 København Ø*

### Sandkaj

Nordhavn is an artificial island built out into the Copenhagen harbour, and is one of the newest swimming spots in the city. A nice boardwalk allows space for a stroll or to sunbathe, and there are plenty of restaurants in the area to get some food or drinks to go. There is also a supermarket right on the boardwalk, so you can stock up on supplies to enjoy a picnic. In winter, many Danes bathe here as well, as there is a sauna by the water.

*Sandkaj 27, 2150 København Ø*

↓ AMAGER STRANDPARK

↓ ISLANDS BRYGGE HARBOUR BATH

↓ AMAGER STRANDPARK

## Islands Brygge Harbour Bath

The Harbour Baths were designed by Bjarke Ingels in 2002, with the goal of creating a safe and clearly marked swimming spot in central Copenhagen. There are multiple pools of different depths, with diving boards. Wooden walkways and ladders make the swimming area one of the most accessible in Copenhagen, and the most popular in summer.

*Islands Brygge 14, 2300 København S*

## Amager Strandpark

Amager Strandpark is a large beachfront area with a range of outdoor recreational opportunities. There are areas for swimming, kayaking, windsurfing, and sandy beaches. There is also a lagoon. Amager Beach Park has a long promenade and breathtaking views of the Øresund Bridge, making it a popular spot. It is also a lovely location for a winter stroll, with a whole range of cafés and food spots. Check out Yellow Bird Coffee (Amager Strandvej 108) for a coffee to boost your walk or have after your swim.

*Amager Strandvej 1, 2300 København S*

# VEGETARIAN AND VEGAN COPENHAGEN

Although Danish cuisine is very meat-and-fish-heavy, there are plenty of options for vegan-friendly and vegetarian cafés and restaurants. Supermarkets also generally have great vegan and plant-based selections.

### Landbageriet

This organic bakery near Nørreport Station sells plenty of vegan options, which are clearly marked. A variety of baked goods is available, including croissants, crispbread, brownies, rolls, and cinnamon buns. Within the bakery, there is also a small grocery shop that sells raw bars, plant-based milk, vegan cheese, and hummus. It's a very tasty and affordable option for breakfast or lunch.

*Frederiksborggade 29, 1360 København K, land-bageriet.dk*

### V'Italian

Conveniently located in a side street of Strøget, this is the perfect place to enjoy some yummy Italian food after shopping. Enjoy antipasti, a steaming plate of pasta, wine, and dessert, all completely vegan. Unlike in some vegan restaurants, the menu is extensive, and has the same choices you would expect from any Italian restaurant.

*Gråbrødretorv 9, 1154 København K, vitalian.dk*

### Vital Foods Café

This café is open for breakfast and lunch, with a range of sandwiches, burritos, and bowls. Their menu has been thoughtfully designed to showcase the vivid hues, tastes, and textures found in nature. Emphasis is placed on the amazing and varied abundance of plant-based ingredients, which range from succulent fruits and vegetables to substantial grains, legumes, and plant-based proteins.

*Kompagnistræde 41, 1208 København K, vitalfoods.dk*

**Bistro Verde**

If you happen to be nearby during the day, stop by for a Spandauer pastry, a traditional pastry with vanilla custard and roasted almonds. Or to try their plant-based take on the traditional cinnamon bun. These are sold until stock runs out, so make sure to get them in the morning. If you plan to come for dinner or lunch, you will see Bistro Verde's plant-based twists on classics such as salmon cream cheese sandwiches, burritos, and burgers. You can also try a spaghetti carbonara with plant-based bacon. Bistro Verde has a small cocktail menu, with wild and sustainable botanicals sourced from Danish nature.

*Sankt Annæ Plads 22, 1250 København K, bistroverdecph.com*

**Ark**

This is the first restaurant in the Nordics to receive a Green Michelin star, which is awarded to restaurants focusing on sustainable gastronomy. Ark also tests the boundaries by focussing on innovation, with new creations entering the menu frequently. The menu features creative dishes made from seasonal, locally sourced ingredients. Each plate is a work of art, showcasing the culinary potential of plant-based cuisine. It is perfect for a special occasion or a memorable (vegan) dining experience.

*Nørre Farimagsgade 63, 1360 København K, restaurantark.dk*

**42 Raw**

In 2009, this was Copenhagen's first establishment with a raw food concept. It is committed to the philosophy that food should be fresh, pure, and unprocessed. The menu is almost fully plant-based, featuring healthy dishes that ensure that the food's nutrients are preserved. You can stop by for a pastry and a juice or sit down for lunch or dinner to enjoy their vegan burgers, raw Pad Thai, and much more.

*ilestrædde 32, 1112 København K, 42raw.com*

**Bistro Lupa**

The brains behind Ark also created Bistro Lupa, a modern bistro focused on plant-based place with a sustainable business model. Like its sister restaurant, Bistro Lupa also received a Green Michelin star. The cocktails are especially tasty, and they are acidified using fermented flavours rather than citrus.

*Marstalsgade 8, 2100 København Ø, bistrolupa.dk*

**VeVe**

This vegetarian restaurant has the same owners as Michelin-starred restaurant Kiin Kiin. It is located by the water near Langelinie and *The Little Mermaid*, in a gorgeous old warehouse. There is a lounge area, and a slightly more formal restaurant area, both decorated with comfortable designer furniture and stylish decor. The menu changes frequently, as there is a focus on seasonal produce. The name VeVe comes from *Vegetarisk Verdenskøkken*, 'vegetarian world cuisine'.

*Dampfærgevej 7, 2100 København Ø, veve.dk*

**Cafe Kaf**

The first vegan bakery in Copenhagen serves sourdough bread, vegan cheesecake, and other baked goods, all 100 per cent plant based. Especially their cinnamon rolls and chocolate croissants are popular, and it is a perfect spot for a leisurely brunch or coffee break.

*Birkegade 21, 2200 København N, cafekaf.dk*

**Nice Cream**

The ice cream at this parlour is 100 per cent vegan, which you wouldn't be able to tell based on its taste or texture. It is made from coconut milk and cane sugar, and often includes banana or other ingredients to ensure it is the yummiest. You can either get a basic ice cream scoop in a cup or a cone, or opt for the more fun, ice-cream sandwich, a scoop of ice cream wedged between two cookies. With a love for the environment, better health for people, and preserving wildlife, they also aim to contribute to a more sustainable industry.

*Elmegade 30, 2200 København N, insta @nicecreamcopenhagen*

**Baka d'Busk**

According to the six friends that call themselves *Plantedrengene* (The Plant Boys) and founded the bistro, when it comes to flavour and texture, plants are far more versatile than meat. Their Insta and YouTube channel show how their playful friendship has manifested itself in great food and an exciting interior. Being at their bistro really is an experience.

*Rantzausgade 44, 2200 København N, insta @baka.d.busk, YouTube @BakadBusk*

**Res-Res**

This is the first shop in Denmark that was B Corp certified, meaning that care for the planet and people is the focus of every decision that they make. Here you can find a Nudie Jeans repair Studio, which offers free repairs for all jeans brought in. Some other popular brands they carry are Veja and Freitag. It can be on the pricier side, but definitely worth a visit, and worth considering buying something more sustainable and planet friendly.

*Guldbergsgade 29 D, 2200 København N, res-res.com*

# OUTSIDE OF COPENHAGEN

Beautiful natural settings, historical landmarks, and artistic treasures abound, and they provide excellent day trips around Copenhagen. Explore contemporary art, historic castles, or picturesque coastlines – these locations provide a welcome escape from the city.

**Louisiana Museum of Modern Art**

*Gammel Strandvej 13, 3050 Humlebæk, louisiana.dk*

Take a fifty-minute train ride to the small village of Humlebæk, where you will find the Louisiana Museum of Modern Art. The museum's extensive collection includes works from artists like Picasso, Warhol, and Hockney. The contemporary and modern artworks are supplemented by the beautiful park, with sculptures and stunning seaside views seamlessly integrating the architecture of the building itself with its natural surroundings.

**Møns Klint**

*Stengårdsvej 8, 4791 Borre, moensklint.dk*

Møns Klint is a striking six-kilometre stretch of white chalk cliffs on the island of Møn's eastern coast. It is a two-hour car ride out of Copenhagen. Climbing to a height of 128 metres above sea level, these magnificent cliffs provide hiking opportunities and breathtaking views. Møns Klint also has an interactive museum, GeoCenter Møns Klint, which allows visitors to learn about the area's geological history.

**Arken Museum for Samtidskunst**

*Skovvej 100, 2635 Ishøj, arken.dk*

Arken Museum of Modern Art is located in Ishøj, along the coast south of Copenhagen. It is known for its architecture, which resembles a stranded ship, and was designed by Søren Robert Lund. The museum is based by Ishøj Harbour and a long sandy beach, so a walk along the dunes is imperative if you visit. Arken also houses one of Europe's best Damien Hirst collections. If you are planning to take a day trip outside of the city, Arken is nice to combine with Møns Klint, as they are close together.

**Kronborg Castle**

*Kronborg, 3000 Helsingør, kronborg.dk*

Kronborg Castle, also known as Elsinore Castle, can be found in Helsingør, which is approximately an hour by train from Copenhagen. This castle is a UNESCO World Heritage site, and the setting for Shakespeare's *Hamlet*. The Renaissance castle overlooks the Øresund Strait and offers various tours of the grounds to learn about the past of the Danish royals.

**The Forgotten Giants**

*thomasdambo.com*

Dispersed throughout forests, meadows, and serene bodies of water in Copenhagen's suburbs are towering, peculiar wood sculptures that are very different from the usual tourist destinations. Undoubtedly off the beaten path are the six municipalities in the greater Copenhagen area that are home to these remarkable works of art. To encourage people to explore and appreciate nature, artist Thomas Dambo chose these picturesque settings for his sculptures

made from recycled wood. The exact locations of the Giants can be found on the website, but you could really immerse yourself in nature and go on a hunt and find them yourself.

**The Forest Tower**

*Skovtårnsvej 1, 4683 Rønnede, campadventure.dk*

The 45-metre Forest Tower is unique, with its hourglass shape. The tower is surrounded by forests, so as you ascend the twelve circles of the spiral structure, you slowly start to encounter a 360-degree view of the towns, ocean, and South Zealand landscape. The building was designed by EFFEKT architects and won several awards before it even opened.

Anno 1849

**Malmö**

*Skovtårnsvej 1, 4683 Rønnede, campadventure.dk*

A mere 45-minute train ride from Copenhagen's central station, you can venture out to neighbouring Sweden for a day trip. Just across the Øresund Bridge lies Malmö, which is a quaint city known for its architecture and beautiful parks. In addition to experiencing Swedish culture as opposed to Danish culture, there are many opportunities for shopping, dining, and cultural experiences. Visit the Turning Torso, a residential, twisting skyscraper which was the second-tallest building in the Nordic region until recently, when the Karlatornet in Gothenburg (Sweden) was built. Malmö Castle, which is only a twenty-minute walk from Malmö central station, is a medieval castle built between 1526 and 1539, making it the oldest preserved Renaissance castle in the Nordic region. Lilla Tort is a little medieval square, next to Stortorget, the big square, which is great to stroll around to visit the lively cafés and restaurants.

# INDEX

# ABOUT THE AUTHOR

**Merel Kernkamp**

Merel is originally Dutch but lived abroad her whole life. During her most formative years, from ages 12-18, she lived in Copenhagen, attending the International School. She is currently studying Law in Amsterdam but hopes to move back to Copenhagen as soon as possible. While living in the quaint neighbourhood of Østerbro, she had the opportunity to explore all corners of the city, often meeting friends for a walk or a coffee, and the occasional night out. She loves to go back to visit her friends who still live there, and greatly contributed with suggestions for this this book. Merel likes to share her love for Copenhagen and her lists of favourites with others, and this book brings them all together.

**WHY SHOULD I GO TO COPENHAGEN**
the city you definitely need to
visit before you turn 30 (or 130)

Published in 2024 by mo'media
P.O. Box 359, 3000 AJ Rotterdam,
The Netherlands, momedia.nl

**Concept**
mo'media

**Text and address selection**
Merel Kernkamp

**Art direction and illustration design**
Jelle F. Post

**Editing**
Ezra van Wilgenburg

**Photography**
Petra de Hamer, David in den Bosch,
mo'media BV and others

**Special thanks to**
Roos & Isa Schulting, Luisa Zaske,
Christina Hjortholm, Ulla Skaaning
Mathiesen, Orla and Emily Damgaard,
and Maaike van Steekelenburg

MIX
Paper from
responsible sources
FSC® C014138

**WHY SHOULD I GO TO?**
Information on all our travel guides
on **WHYSHOULDIGOTO.COM**



Why Should I Go To Copenhagen
ISBN 978 94 9333 845 6
NUR 510

**Disclaimer**
The points of interested mentioned in this travel guide have been selected by the author. None of them have been paid for inclusion in this book: the *Why Should I Go To* book series is entirely ad-free.

**Publisher's Note**
Every effort has been made to ensure that the information in this book is accurate at the time of going to press. The publisher welcomes any information or suggestions for correction or improvement. Please send us an e-mail at info@momedia.nl or a DM on Instagram.

whyshouldigoto

**Why Should I Go To travel guides are available for the following cities:** Amsterdam, Antwerp, Barcelona, Berlin, Copenhagen, London, Paris, and Prague. More cities will be added soon. Check our socials for updates.

In this skillfully edited edition, Randall Pederson has chosen passages drawn from George Whitefield's sermons, letters, hymns, and prayers that will encourage, inspire and challenge the reader each day of the year. This is the first devotional compiled solely from Whitefield's works and provides an excellent introduction to the spirituality of this eighteenth-century evangelical preacher who was so used by God in bringing the gospel into the lives of so many people both in the UK and USA. Bible passages are based upon the ESV.

# Sample

## JANUARY 26

### Tasting Christ's Love

*Greater love has no one than this, that someone lay down his life for his friends.*

JOHN 15:13

If you are zealous for the Lord and seek Jesus, if your zeal is according to godliness, and you pray to him for his Spirit, you shall certainly have an answer of peace; you shall find it is good to seek the Lord, you will be adopted into his family, and by his Spirit be enabled to cry, "Abba, Father." O then, do not leave, but be continually waiting at wisdom's gate, and you shall find

CHRISTIAN HERITAGE
*Useful Books of Lasting Value*
CHRISTIAN FOCUS PUBLICATIONS
www.christianfocus.com

ISBN 978-1-84550-580-6
9 781845 505806
Devotional, BISAC - REL012020 | UK£19.99 US$25.99